The United Nations De
Programme and System

D1454579

LIBRARY

TO BE
DISPOSED
BY
AUTHORITY

Stats

1 9 DEC 2011

House of Commons Library

54056001219515

This volume provides a short, accessible introduction to the organization that serves as the primary coordinator of the work of the UN system throughout the developing world—the United Nations Development Programme (UNDP).

The book:

- traces the origins and evolution of UNDP, outlining how a central UN funding mechanism and field network developed into a more comprehensive development agency;
- evaluates the UNDP's performance and results, both in its role as system coordinator and as a development organization in its own right; and
- considers the return of the UNDP to a more central role within the UN development system, in order to review the successive attempts at UN development system reform, the reasons for failure, and the future possibilities for a more effective system with UNDP at the center.

Offering a clear, comprehensive overview and analysis of the organization, this work will be of great interest to students and scholars of development studies, international organizations, and international relations.

Stephen Browne is Director of The Future of the UN Development System (FUNDS) Project and Fellow of the Ralph Bunche Institute for International Studies at the Graduate Center of the City University of New York.

Routledge Global Institutions Series
Edited by Thomas G. Weiss
The CUNY Graduate Center, New York, USA
and Rorden Wilkinson
University of Manchester, UK

About the series

The Global Institutions Series is designed to provide readers with comprehensive, accessible, and informative guides to the history, structure, and activities of key international organizations as well as books that deal with topics of key importance in contemporary global governance. Every volume stands on its own as a thorough and insightful treatment of a particular topic, but the series as a whole contributes to a coherent and complementary portrait of the phenomenon of global institutions at the dawn of the millennium.

Books are written by recognized experts, conform to a similar structure, and cover a range of themes and debates common to the series. These areas of shared concern include the general purpose and rationale for organizations, developments over time, membership, structure, decision-making procedures, and key functions. Moreover, current debates are placed in historical perspective alongside informed analysis and critique. Each book also contains an annotated bibliography and guide to electronic information as well as any annexes appropriate to the subject matter at hand.

The volumes currently published are:

57 The United Nations Development Programme and System (2011)
by Stephen Browne (FUNDS Project)

56 The South Asian Association for Regional Cooperation (2011)
An emerging collaboration architecture
by Lawrence Sáez (University of London)

55 The UN Human Rights Council (2011)
by Bertrand G. Ramcharan (Geneva Graduate Institute of International and Development Studies)

Books currently under contract include:

The Regional Development Banks
Lending with a regional flavor
by Jonathan R. Strand (University of Nevada)

Millennium Development Goals (MDGs)
For a people-centered development agenda?
by Sakiko Fukada-Parr (The New School)

Peacebuilding
From concept to commission
by Robert Jenkins (The CUNY Graduate Center)

Human Security
by Don Hubert (University of Ottawa)

UNICEF
by Richard Jolly (University of Sussex)

FIFA
by Alan Tomlinson (University of Brighton)

International Law, International Relations, and Global Governance
by Charlotte Ku (University of Illinois)

The Bank for International Settlements
The politics of global financial supervision in the age of high finance
by Kevin Ozgercin (SUNY College at Old Westbury)

International Migration
by Khalid Koser (Geneva Centre for Security Policy)

Global Health Governance
by Sophie Harman (City University, London)

The Council of Europe
by Martyn Bond (University of London)

Human Development
by Richard Ponzio

Religious Institutions and Global Politics
by Katherine Marshall (Georgetown University)

The Group of Twenty (G20)
by Andrew F. Cooper (Centre for International Governance Innovation, Ontario) and Ramesh Thakur (Balsillie School of International Affairs, Ontario)

The International Monetary Fund (2nd edition)
Politics of conditional lending
by James Raymond Vreeland (Georgetown University)

The UN Global Compact
by Catia Gregoratti (Lund University)

Security Governance in Regional Organizations
edited by Emil Kirchner (University of Essex) and Roberto Dominguez (Suffolk University)

UN Institutions for Women's Rights
by Charlotte Patton (York College, CUNY) and Carolyn Stephenson (University of Hawaii)

International Aid
by Paul Mosley (University of Sheffield)

Maritime Piracy
by Bob Haywood and Roberta Spivak

For further information regarding the series, please contact:
Craig Fowlie, Publisher, Politics & International Studies
Taylor & Francis
2 Park Square, Milton Park, Abingdon
Oxford OX14 4RN, UK
+44 (0)207 842 2057 Tel
+44 (0)207 842 2302 Fax
Craig.Fowlie@tandf.co.uk
www.routledge.com

The United Nations Development Programme and System

Stephen Browne

Routledge
Taylor & Francis Group

LONDON AND NEW YORK

First published 2011
by Routledge
2 Park Square, Milton Park, Abingdon, Oxon, OX14 4RN

Simultaneously published in the USA and Canada
by Routledge
711 Third Avenue, New York, NY 10017

Routledge is an imprint of the Taylor & Francis Group, an informa business

© 2011 Stephen Browne
The right of Stephen Browne to be identified as author of this work has been asserted by him in accordance with the Copyright, Designs and Patent Act 1988.

All rights reserved. No part of this book may be reprinted or reproduced or utilised in any form or by any electronic, mechanical, or other means, now known or hereafter invented, including photocopying and recording, or in any information storage or retrieval system, without permission in writing from the publishers.

Trademark notice: Product or corporate names may be trademarks or registered trademarks, and are used only for identification and explanation without intent to infringe.

British Library Cataloguing in Publication Data
A catalogue record for this book is available from the British Library

Library of Congress Cataloging in Publication Data
The United Nations Development Programme and System/ Stephen Browne.
    p. cm. – (Routledge global institutions series; 57)
    Includes bibliographical references and index.
    1. United Nations Development Programme. 2. United Nations – Economic assistance. 3. United Nations – Technical assistance.
    I. Title.
    JZ4972.B76 2011
    343'.07 – dc22   2011004444

ISBN: 978-0-415-77649-3 (hbk)
ISBN: 978-0-415-77650-9 (pbk)
ISBN: 978-0-203-80685-2 (ebk)

Typeset in Times New Roman
by Taylor & Francis Books

MIX
Paper from
responsible sources
FSC
www.fsc.org FSC® C004839

Printed and bound in Great Britain by
TJ International Ltd, Padstow, Cornwall

Contents

Illustrations

Figures

Tables

Boxes

Foreword by the series editors

The current volume is the fifty-seventh title in a dynamic series on global institutions. These books provide readers with definitive guides to the most visible aspects of what many of us know as "global governance." Remarkable as it may seem, there exist relatively few books that offer in-depth treatments of prominent global bodies, processes, and associated issues, much less an entire series of concise and complementary volumes. Those that do exist are either out of date, inaccessible to the non-specialist reader, or seek to develop a specialized understanding of particular aspects of an institution or process rather than offer an overall account of its functioning and situate it within the increasingly dense global institutional network. Similarly, existing books have often been written in highly technical language, or have been crafted "in-house" and are notoriously self-serving and narrow.

The advent of electronic media has undoubtedly helped research and teaching by making data and primary documents of international organizations more widely available, but it has complicated matters as well. The growing reliance on the Internet and other electronic methods of finding information about key international organizations and processes has served, ironically, to limit the educational and analytical materials to which most readers have ready access—namely, books. Public relations documents, raw data, and loosely refereed websites do not make for intelligent analysis. Official publications compete with a vast amount of electronically available information, much of which is suspect because of its ideological or self-promoting slant. Paradoxically, a growing range of purportedly independent websites offering analyses of the activities of particular organizations has emerged, but one inadvertent consequence has been to frustrate access to basic, authoritative, readable, critical, and well-researched texts. The market for such has actually been reduced by the ready availability of electronic materials of varying quality.

For those of us who teach, research, and operate in the area, such restricted access to information and analyses has been frustrating. We were delighted when Routledge saw the value of a series that bucks this trend and provides key reference points to the most significant global institutions and issues. They are betting that serious students and professionals will want serious analyses. We have assembled a first-rate team of authors to address that market. Our intention is to provide one-stop shopping for all readers—students (both undergraduate and postgraduate), negotiators, diplomats, practitioners from nongovernmrntal and intergovernmental organizations, and interested parties alike—seeking insights into the most prominent institutional aspects of global governance.

The United Nations Development Programme and System

The Preamble to the United Nations Charter is clear about its central purpose, "to save succeeding generations from the scourge of war." Rising from the ashes of the second worldwide devastation within three decades, the founders clearly emphasized the imperative to address international peace and security. "The promotion of economic and social advancement" for colonized peoples and what soon were to become known as "underdeveloped countries" was viewed as a means to ensure international peace and security.

The liberation and independence of the globe's dependent peoples turned development into a valid end in itself rather than a means to help ensure the peace. And after the Cold War paralyzed the UN Security Council, economic and social development became *the* business of the UN system.

This Global Institutions Series already contains a host of books on the component parts of what is known as the "UN development system," and so we are truly pleased finally to have a book that we have always thought would be central to understanding the complexities of the various moving parts in the UN's organigram, which all contribute in specialized ways to the promotion of economic and social advancement. Here, between two covers, the reader has not only a map of the system, but also an overview of the nuts and bolts of the organization that, since its founding in 1966, has sought to provide overall coordination and funding—the UN Development Programme (UNDP).

We are delighted that Stephen Browne agreed to write this much needed volume that covers the UNDP and the development system as well. Stephen has over three decades of experience within the United

Nations system, including his last position as Deputy Executive Director of the International Trade Centre, which resulted in an earlier book in the series.[1] He is an unusual practitioner who found time to write while a UN official three other books on development assistance.[2] Currently he is director of The Future of the UN Development System (FUNDS) Project and Fellow of the Ralph Bunche Institute for International Studies at The Graduate Center of The City University of New York. This book benefits immensely from Stephen's efforts to document and make sense of the activities of the 50,000 staff members and the $20 billion annual expenditure currently being spent across the decentralized UN development system.

We are delighted to have this book in the series because it enriches the literature on global institutions and governance. We wholeheartedly recommend it and, as always, welcome comments from our readers.

Thomas G. Weiss, The CUNY Graduate Center, New York, USA
Rorden Wilkinson, University of Manchester, UK
February 2011

Foreword by Craig Murphy

What is the United Nations?

To many people in the United States or in Western Europe, the answer is simple: it is the club of national governments that meets in New York and Geneva, a talking-shop, a venue for high-sounding rhetoric, and (occasionally) some serious diplomatic work.

For people in many other countries—places where people are apt to come into contact with men and women who work for the UN, or at least to see them on TV—the answer tends to be different. The answer will be that the UN *is* those people hired or seconded to the UN, what scholars call "the Second United Nations," the 99,000 peacekeepers, 130,000 civilian field staff, and perhaps even the 34,000 staffers back in Western Europe or North America at the headquarters, to whom the field workers report.[1]

This United Nations is all about the developing world. Almost all the peacekeepers are there, and all but about 6,000 (6 percent) of them come from there, as well. All of the field offices are in the developing world or in Eastern European "transition countries," and 83 percent of them are locally recruited. The headquarters' staffs have much higher percentages of people from the developed world. (As a 40-year veteran local staff member in India once told me, "The UN is very much a big organization of brown people topped by a small group of white men.") Still, the work of almost half the headquarters' staffers across the organizations, from the Food and Agricultural Organization to the World Meteorological Organization, is directed toward the developing world. In any objective sense, "the UN system" and "the UN development system" are almost coterminous.

This book is about the civilian side of the UN development system. The book focuses on the organization that has always been the only real provider of coherence across the system—the UN Development Programme (UNDP)—which, today, still provides most of the UN Resident Coordinators (who try to herd the UN cats in the field) and whose boss in New York (the "Administrator," a wonderfully understated title that goes back to the Marshall Plan) heads the headquarters-focused "UN Development Group." Even so, the book is not just about the civilian side of things, simply because so many of the men and women who have served the Secretary-General as his "Special Representative" (i.e. UN chief) in countries in conflict have risen through UNDP.

Stephen Browne is perhaps the person best placed to write about UNDP within the context of the entire UN development system. Browne had a distinguished 23-year career within the UNDP, serving in Rwanda during its post-genocide reconstruction as head of what was then one of the Programme's largest country offices, and earlier as the first UN Representative in Ukraine, directing a well-meant (but, unfortunately, terminated) experiment of having the entire UN system operating as a single entity at the country level.

Browne is more than just a distinguished administrator; he is a well-recognized critical scholar of the development enterprise, someone inspired by the World Bank's most distinguished Vice Presidents for Research—Mahbub ul Haq (later, founder of UNDP's Human Development Office), Hollis Chenery, and Larry Summers—and UNICEF's Richard Jolly, but, unlike the works of these men, Browne's major books and articles have focused less on what might be the ideal, "right" development policy for a particular country, and more on how the political economy of the global development system, and the resulting peculiarities of its governance, create real obstacles to development.

Browne is no cheerleader for the development enterprise as it now exists, as this book's critiques of UNDP's sometimes misguided efforts makes clear, but he is a champion of the idea that rational reflection on the experience of more than 60 years of international development assistance should allow us to improve on what has been done. Since he left the UN system in 2009, he has led a significant attempt to analyze and reform the UN development system—The Future of the UN Development System (FUNDS) Project—which is bringing together heads of UN organizations, representatives of major donors, scholars, management professionals, and civil society groups throughout the world to create a comprehensive, workable blueprint for a radically improved system.

This book grew out of that project, and has been informed by Browne's entire career. It provides a concise, comprehensive, forward-looking picture of UNDP and the larger system of which it is a part. It is one of the first resources for anyone concerned with understanding that system and making it more effective.

Craig N. Murphy, Professor of Global Governance, University of Massachusetts Boston and M. Margaret Ball Professor of International Relations, Wellesley College, Massachusetts

Acknowledgments

I wish to acknowledge the valuable and detailed material made available to me by Craig Murphy, UNDP historian (2004–2006), who was not the first to encounter the challenges presented by the absence of any comprehensive electronic memory in the organization. The draft also benefited from conversations which I had with a past Administrator, Mark Malloch Brown, and with the current one, Helen Clark. Useful written comments were provided by Richard Jolly, Siba Das, Saraswathi Menon, and Leelananda de Silva. Having spent more than three decades in the UN development system, I am also indebted to colleagues—far too numerous to mention—in widely dispersed headquarters and field locations, with whom I have had lively and enriching interactions over many years on the present and future of the UN.

Chapter 5 has also benefited from the insights of participants at a conference on the Future of the UN Development System, held at Wilton Park in the United Kingdom in November 2010.

Finally, special thanks go to the staff of the UN Library in the Palais des Nations, Geneva (Carla, Cristina, and Carlos Adriano), who efficiently located even the more obscure UN official documents that could not be found online; and vicariously to John D. Rockefeller, who had the extraordinary wisdom to fund the creation of the six-story building whose resources I mined in depth in writing this book.

The judgments and facts presented in the book nevertheless remain my sole responsibility.

Stephen Browne

Abbreviations

ASEAN	Association of South-East Asian Nations
BCPR	Bureau for Crisis Prevention and Recovery
BDP	Bureau for Development Policy
CEB	Chief Executives Board (UN)
CFCs	chlorofluorocarbons
DAC	(OECD) Development Assistance Committee
DFID	Department for International Development (UK)
DOT	Digital Opportunities Task-force
EC	European Commission
ECA	UN Economic Commission for Africa
ECE	UN Economic Commission for Europe
ECLA(C)	UN Economic Commission for Latin America (and the Caribbean)
ECOSOC	Economic and Social Council of the UN
ECOWAS	Economic Community of West African States
EPTA	Expanded Programme of Technical Assistance
ESCAP	UN Economic and Social Commission for Asia and the Pacific
ESCWA	UN Economic Commission for West Asia
EU	European Union
FAO	Food and Agriculture Organization of the UN
G77	Group of 77 developing countries and China
GATT	General Agreement on Tariffs and Trade
GEF	Global Environment Facility
GFATM	Global Fund for AIDS, Tuberculosis and Malaria
HDI	Human Development Index
HDR	Human Development Report
HPI	Human Poverty Index
ICANN	Internet Corporation for Assigned Names and Numbers
ICAO	International Civil Aviation Organization

ICT	information and communication technologies
IDA	International Development Authority (UN); International Development Association (World Bank)
IFAD	International Fund for Agricultural Development (UN)
ILO	International Labour Organization
IMF	International Monetary Fund
IMO	International Maritime Organization
IPF	Indicative Planning Figure
ISO	International Organization for Standardization
ITC	International Trade Centre
ITU	International Telecommunications Union
LDC	least developed country
MDGs	Millennium Development Goals
MESC	Middle-East Service Centre
MOPAN	Multilateral Organization Performance Assessment Network
MYFF	Multi-Year Funding Framework
NEX	national execution
NGO	nongovernmental organization
NIEO	new international economic order
OAU	Organization for African Unity
OECD	Organization for Economic Cooperation and Development
OEOA	UN Office for Emergency Operations in Africa
OPE	Office of Project Execution (later UNOPS)
OPEX	Operational and Executive Personnel
PRSP	Poverty Reduction Strategy Paper
RBM	results-based management
RCM	regional coordination mechanism
RDT	regional director team
ROAR	results-oriented annual reports
SBAA	Standard Basic Assistance Agreement
SDA	Social Dimensions of Adjustment (World Bank program)
SHD	sustainable human development
SUNFED	Special UN Fund for Economic Development
SuRF	sub-regional resource facility
TA	technical assistance
TAA	Technical Assistance Administration
TAB	Technical Assistance Board
TAC	Technical Assistance Committee
TOKTEN	Transfer of Knowledge Through Expatriate Nationals program

UN	United Nations
UN DESA	UN Department of Economic and Social Affairs
UNAIDS	Joint UN Programme on HIV/AIDS
UNCDF	UN Capital Development Fund
UNCTAD	UN Conference on Trade and Development
UNDG	UN Development Group
UNDOCO	UN Development Operations Coordination Office
UNDP	UN Development Programme
UNEP	UN Environment Programme
UNESC	UN Economic and Social Security Council (proposed)
UNESCO	UN Educational, Scientific and Cultural Organization
UNFPA	UN Population Fund (formerly UN Fund for Population Activities)
UNFSSTD	UN Financing System for Science and Technology for Development
UN-HABITAT	UN Human Settlements Programme
UNHCR	UN High Commission for Refugees
UNICEF	UN Children's Fund
UNIDO	UN Industrial Development Organization
UNIFEM	UN Fund for Women (UNDP)
UNOPS	UN Office for Project Services (formerly OPE)
UNRRA	UN Relief and Rehabilitation Administration
UNSO	UN Sahelian Office (later Drylands Development Centre)
UNV	UN Volunteers
UNWTO	World Tourism Organization
UPU	Universal Postal Union
WFP	World Food Programme (UN)
WHO	World Health Organization
WIPO	World Intellectual Property Organization
WRI	World Resources Institute
WTO	World Trade Organization

Introduction

- **UNDP's original purpose**
- **Free technical assistance and its consequences**
- **From fund to development organization**

This is the story of an organization that gave up the role for which it was originally created, discovered a different one, and then partially returned to its original functions, thus pursuing a double identity within a complex and disparate UN development system.

UNDP's original purpose

In the immediate aftermath of the Second World War, a unity beyond politics provided a propitious environment for global technical exchange. Economic and social advancement promised to consolidate the peace and was written into the new UN Charter. In the name of functional cooperation,[1] a host of new and revived international organizations were brought into the lee of the UN as a means of meeting the technical needs of what were termed the "undeveloped areas."[2]

Needs were perceived in strict compartments. The technical agencies brought together specialists in each respective field to collaborate on specific technical solutions: health in the World Health Organization (WHO); agriculture in the Food and Agriculture Organization of the UN (FAO); science and education in the UN Educational, Scientific and Cultural Organization (UNESCO); civil aviation in the International Civil Aviation Organization (ICAO)—all agencies created between 1945 and 1948.[3] The importance and universality of technical solutions to the challenges of the time vested them with a degree of importance and sufficiency that was resistant to larger binding frameworks.

So the inchoate UN development system was not a family within which the members interacted, but a collection of agencies with only an emblem in common, albeit one that signified universality. Only later did it become evident that progress demanded more holistic, "multi-sectoral" approaches. But by then there were several independent, maturing organizational structures, making it difficult to envisage the architecture for a single edifice.

This was the background against which two funding mechanisms emerged within the UN. The first, and more innocuous, was a facility intended to expand opportunities for the transfer of expertise from the advanced to the developing countries, for which a major inspiration was the 1949 inaugural speech of US President Harry Truman. The speech was important because it signified a change of heart. Until that moment, even the notion of a UN-controlled fund was unpopular. Indeed non-humanitarian aid through multilateral channels was itself controversial because it was beyond the direct control of the funders. For the United States—the only country in a position to provide significant support—the doubts about multilateral aid were only enhanced as the Cold War entrenched rival spheres of influence.

The Expanded Programme of Technical Assistance (EPTA) was therefore a modest compromise, designed to facilitate the transfer of expertise via the UN. But for nearly the whole of the 1950s, the UN's continuing attempts to launch a much larger development finance initiative were strongly resisted by the United States and the United Kingdom in particular. Free advice was one thing, but free money was anathema to the two countries whose banks dominated global finance. Eventually, multilateral aid won out, but the main prize was given to the safe hands of the World Bank, in which the rich countries were the dominant shareholders. A "special fund" on a more modest scale was awarded to the UN on the understanding that one of its main purposes was pre-investment—a means to identify bankable projects.

UNDP—the offspring of both EPTA and the special fund—was thus born into a doubly challenging environment. It was intended to facilitate comprehensive development solutions by mobilizing technical assistance (TA) from a range of organizations that had sought to safeguard their autonomy from the outset. And it was an instrument of development assistance with controversial origins. The problems stemming from global development welfare have never gone away.

Free technical assistance and its consequences

Chapter 1 mentions the earliest examples of multilateral TA, organized in the health field under the auspices of the League of Nations.

Pre-revolutionary China was the main recipient, but it was also the *demandeur* in the commercial sense and paid for all the expertise, as well as for the League's presence in the country. Before the Second World War, there were many other examples of countries requesting and purchasing specialized expertise from abroad. Technical assistance was essentially part of a bilateral commercial transaction.[4]

The idea of offering free services—especially on the scale which it soon took on—was a new and specifically non-commercial idea, passing between two public sectors. In the early days of TA, the requesting government was expected to pay part of the costs, or at least to make counterpart resources available. Within the UN, there were well-designed schemes to ensure services were exchanged for resources put up by the governments of developing countries. They are described in Chapter 1. But, for the emerging bilateral programs, free assistance was a means of influence as well as support, and "free TA" quickly became ingrained as an entirely natural basis for all development cooperation. Even though newly independent developing countries could easily have afforded to buy the expertise they needed, they were not asked to (except for modest project counterpart costs). Aid was pre-paid and, for several decades afterwards, TA from all bilateral and multilateral sources was free under aid programs. Some developing countries paid for similar services from commercial sources, in addition to what they received free of charge. But most recipient countries were persuaded to believe that they could not have managed without this increasingly elaborate system of development welfare.[5]

The idea of "free" assistance is so ingrained that it is now rarely questioned. But the distortions associated with pre-paid assistance are legion. In bilateral programs, TA reflects what donors are best placed to provide, and may not coincide with developing country needs. This leads to problems of ownership: whose aid is it, and which party really benefits?[6] Free TA also draws away resources in patterns that favor donor-inspired projects. Then there is the problem of dependence. When donors supply solutions, whether in the form of technical services, equipment, or systems of any kind, recipient countries become familiar with and dependent on them: equipment needs spare parts from the same supplier; a particular training scheme depends on a specific group of trainers, and so on. There is also the more general, and more perilous, behavioral dependence that results from the ongoing provision of "free" TA. Recipient countries come to believe that all problems can—and therefore should—be tackled through foreign solutions. Dependence on free solutions has persistently inhibited the development of home-grown capacity.

Multilateral aid shares many of these distortions. Chapter 1 describes the cost-sharing schemes developed by the UN in the early days. But the system could scarcely have charged for its services when similar assistance was being provided free from bilateral sources, and these schemes were soon abandoned. (The automatic funding entitlements from EPTA insisted on by UN agencies also provided a poor example of easy charity.)

Subsequently, supply-sidedness has allowed donor interests to exert considerable influence. These interests were filtered through UN agency and organization secretariats, which developed programs reflecting their own preferences, but which they also judged to be appealing to their main benefactors. One of the most respected UNDP pioneers, Joan Anstee, once remarked that "any relationship between the program and the priority needs of a developing country is purely coincidental."[7] Several decades later, one of the UN's chroniclers described the distortions thus: "... ambiguity about sovereignty has all along characterized the aid relationship, especially aid through the UN system. In actuality, the agencies that determined and implemented the aid have had a strong, even decisive, influence not only on who received the assistance but also on the purposes it served and the principles that governed its implementation."[8] With free aid, developing countries do not necessarily get what they want; they get what donors, and the agencies they fund, want them to have.

As non-core (i.e. earmarked) funding from donor countries for UN development has grown, so have the structural distortions. UNDP and the rest of the system were encouraged to expand in some areas, even when the interests of developing countries in those areas had not been strongly manifested. Dependence on a limited number of donors also carries risks, as it exposes the UN to funding vagaries provoked by domestic policy considerations in those donor countries. Funding can suddenly decline and activities ("supply") decrease, even though development needs ("demand") are growing.

In the multilateral context, dependence takes on larger and potentially debilitating dimensions. The global community is a huge, heterogeneous family of states with widely differing endowments, development levels and challenges. Each country and its problems are unique. Yet, in the UN context, member states are labeled either "developed" donors (North), or "developing" recipients (South). The latter heterogeneous grouping is called the "G77 and China" and often negotiates in policy forums as an indivisible bloc. They have virtually nothing in common except the fact that they are aid recipients. Thus the arguments are always focused on aid. In every UN development forum, global or regional, this simplistic Manichaean division prevails, often to the exclusion of a more meaningful debate about issues. Aid as patronage—and the identification of aid with development solutions—has conditioned development thinking to such an extent that the UN's global conferences during the 1990s invariably ended with sterile wrangling over amounts of new assistance.[9]

As this book chronicles, the strength of North–South patronage in UNDP and the UN system grew steadily as the "foreign aid business"[10] expanded in size and sophistication. Today, non-core funding makes up 59 percent of the contributions through the UN development system.[11] For UNDP, the proportion is no less than 80 percent. Since the 1990s, however, a potentially welcome trend has been a rise in non-core contributions to UNDP—and, to a smaller extent, some of the agencies—from the middle-income countries of Latin America, in return for administrative and procurement services. Even more recently, UNDP has begun to rediscover its earlier role as a central funding mechanism of the UN system through the management of a growing number of multi-donor and multi-agency trust funds. To some extent, therefore, UNDP has begun to rediscover its funding roots, both as a recipient of funds from developing countries—which had been a feature of EPTA—and as a funding source for the benefit of the system as a whole.

From fund to development organization

When EPTA and the Special Fund were merged into UNDP in 1965, the UN development system had a consolidated source of resources to finance its TA programs. But UNDP and the family of its UN executing agencies soon discovered they could easily do without each other, thus expunging UNDP's original rationale as a funder and consolidator of the system. UNDP—as well as the other agencies and organizations—continued to solicit funding from the same donors, but began to diversify its spending away from the UN system. A growing proportion of the core funds allocated to individual developing countries became "nationally executed," which meant in practice that UNDP offices had a major influence on how the money was spent. UNDP created its own executing arm—the Office for Project Execution—through which a significant proportion of funding was initially channeled. But implementation became increasingly diversified. As UNDP became more successful at attracting non-core funds (which are beyond the direct scrutiny of the official governance machinery), they were spent on its own in-house programs, including large numbers of project staff.

From system consolidator and coordinator, UNDP thus became a full-service development organization of its own. Since it competed with the rest of the system, both to attract funds from the same donors, and to implement programs in some of the same domains, UNDP could no longer be considered a credible center of the system, as had originally been intended. UNDP nevertheless managed to retain a coordinating role at the country level, not as the senior service, but as a *primus inter pares*, a role necessitated by the proliferation of UN system field representatives—now numbering 1,022 offices[12]—which accompanied UNDP's transformation into a development organization.

Over the next three chapters, this book tracks the origins and evolution of UNDP, outlining how a central UN funding mechanism and field network developed into a more comprehensive development agency. Chapter 4 reviews UNDP's performance and results, both in its role as system coordinator and as a development organization in its own right. Chapter 5, the final chapter, places UNDP back into the context of the UN development system, within which it has always played a key—albeit somewhat ambiguous—role. It reviews the successive attempts at UN development system reform, the reasons for failure, and the possibilities for a future, more effective system with UNDP back at the center.

The book ends almost where it began. The experience of more than 60 years of development has helped to reconfirm that the UN development system's past contains many lessons for its future.

1   The origins of UNDP

- The origins of UN technical assistance
- The Expanded Programme of Technical Assistance
- The Special Fund
- OPEX and the principles of partnership
- The birth of UNDP
- The Capacity Study
- The system is dead, long live the system ...
- New dimensions for UNDP
- New programs
- The golden partnership

The creation of UNDP was motivated by a post-war logic that the developing countries needed TA from a multilateral source to fill the gaps in institutions and skills required by what was, at the time, still an ill-defined development process. There were no antecedents for this kind of "free" multilateral assistance, and it took a sudden change of heart by a US president to open the way to the creation of the Expanded Programme of Technical Assistance (EPTA), the forerunner of UNDP. The EPTA helped establish the practice of pre-funded aid from multilateral and bilateral sources—a form of top-down patronage that is now taken for granted.

This chapter traces the origins of UNDP from the immediate post-war period, its formal birth in 1965 and its subsequent evolution up to the 1970s. An important part of the story has been the unsuccessful attempt to cement UNDP's role at the center of the UN development system.

The origins of UN technical assistance

UNDP started life in January 1965 as a result of a merger of two existing funding programs: EPTA, created in 1950; and the Special Fund of 1959.[1] The origins of each were themselves the result of a protracted debate about the role of the UN in development cooperation, and multilateral assistance in general.

The earliest example of multilateral TA was almost certainly under the League of Nations in the 1930s, for which provision was made under the League's Covenant.[2] An example was a request from China for advisory assistance on health and hygiene. Given the delicacies of the political situation at the time in the region—with the Sino-Japanese conflict breaking out in 1931—and Chinese concerns over sovereignty, acceding to the request took time to negotiate. Experts were sent on the strict understanding that their role was to advise rather than decide. In 1933, the first resident technical adviser was installed—a forerunner of the UN country representatives. By 1941, some 30 advisers had been fielded, all paid for by the Chinese government.[3]

The next examples of multilateral assistance were of a humanitarian nature, as a response to the devastation of the Second World War and the need to resettle six million displaced people in Europe. The UN Relief and Rehabilitation Administration (UNRRA) was established in 1943, drawing staff from the successful Middle East Service Centre (MESC), created by the British to support the economies of that region. One of these was Robert Jackson, a towering personality in the early history of the United Nations. An Australian from a military background, he had made his name during the war through his work with the MESC, which became something of a model for later UN TA. Jackson went on to become deputy head of the UNRRA, and subsequently played several key roles under the authority of the UN Secretary-General.[4] He was later to play an important part in fashioning the architecture of the UNDP.

UNRRA had a very clearly circumscribed mandate, and by 1947 it was wound up—a rare occurrence of organizational demise in the UN. Its fate was determined by ideology and the onset of the Cold War. Some in the US Congress would not countenance a United States-backed agency prepared to provide assistance to the Communist bloc in Europe.[5] The UN was nevertheless able to redirect UNRRA's remaining funds to several of the new agencies to support their humanitarian and TA activities, including FAO (1945), UNESCO (1945), UNICEF (1946),[6] and WHO (1948).

When it came to drafting the UN Charter, some in the developed country delegations were reluctant to give economic and social issues the same priority as political issues.[7] However, enlightened opinion won out in San Francisco, and the Charter's language was explicit about the international organization's role in supporting development. Article 55 stipulated the promotion of:

- higher standards of living, full employment, and conditions of economic and social progress and development;
- solutions of international economic, social, health and related problems; and international cultural and educational cooperation; and
- universal respect for, and observance of, human rights and fundamental freedoms for all without distinction as to race, sex, language or religion.

How was all this to be achieved? The specialized agencies were being provided with modest sums in their regular budgets for TA in their respective fields. In 1946, the UN Organization itself—the secretariat under the immediate authority of the Secretary-General—was allowed a small fund in its own regular budget in 1946 to undertake "advisory social welfare services," a domain not covered by the mandates of the agencies. In 1948, the scope of these services was expanded to include economic development and public administration. Much more significant, however, was the agreement in the UN's main development committee, the Economic and Social Council (ECOSOC) in August 1949 to establish the Expanded Programme of Technical Assistance for Economic Development, with a significantly larger appropriation.[8]

The Expanded Programme of Technical Assistance

The birth of EPTA had been a matter of some debate. The aid discussion at the time was dominated by the United States, which was the only country in the 1940s in a position to provide substantial amounts of assistance, as it demonstrated with its approval of the Marshall Plan in 1948. Many in the United States were more reluctant about multilateral assistance, over which they could exert little direct control. One of the initial detractors was President Truman. However, he evidently changed his mind. In his inaugural address of January 1949, where he adumbrated US foreign policy in four points, he committed America in the first to support the UN and the specialized agencies. In the fourth, he stated:

> [...] we must embark on a bold new program for making the benefits of our scientific advances and industrial progress available for the improvement and growth of under-developed areas [...] we should make available to peace-loving peoples the benefits of our store of technical knowledge in order to help them realize their aspirations for a better life. And in cooperation with other nations, we should foster capital investment in areas needing development. [...] we invite other countries to pool their technological resources

in this undertaking [...] This should be a cooperative enterprise in which all nations work together through the United Nations and its specialized agencies wherever practical.[9]

It was a clarion call for the UN. Shortly afterwards, the secretariat, with the collaboration of the specialized agencies, drew up a detailed proposal leading to the approval of EPTA that same year as a fund for a full range of TA activities. The EPTA resolution also provided guidelines on the governance and administration of the new program. ECOSOC would establish a Technical Assistance Committee (TAC) to oversee a Technical Assistance Board (TAB), chaired by the Secretary-General and comprising the heads of the specialized agencies (Figure 1.1). The TAB would be responsible for receiving requests for assistance and passing these on for approval by the TAC. In the first pledging conference in June 1950, donors provided $20 million to EPTA. It was below the ambitious target of the UN, but it was a solid start.

A key figure in this exercise was David Owen, reputedly the first person to be recruited to the UN secretariat after the war, and at the time head of the Economic Department. He coordinated the preparatory meetings for EPTA and oversaw the drafting of the blueprint. He was to become the Executive Secretary of the new TAB, and subsequently its Executive Chairman.

One of Owen's main challenges in guiding the early stages of EPTA was the thorny problem of apportioning funds to the agencies. They were designated as beneficiaries of the new funds and they wanted to be sure of safeguarding their shares. Partly it was a matter of organizational ambition. But there was a practical need to ensure continuity in the management and staffing of their TA programs. There was protracted debate on the apportionments, which were initially among five agencies (FAO, UNESCO, WHO, the International Labour Organization (ILO), and ICAO) and the UN itself, which had established its own Technical Assistance Administration (TAA) within the secretariat, headed by a director-general. Shares were finally agreed through a clumsy process of compromise, which had as much to do with the persuasive powers of the agencies as with any more dispassionate overview of contemporary development needs. Balance is difficult in any multilateralism system. However, giving guarantees to the agencies was clearly at odds with the aspirations of developing countries to present proposals to EPTA for funding based on their own specific development priorities. During the TAC meetings in 1953, which reviewed the start-up of the new organization, Owen remarked that "logically it was extremely difficult to reconcile integrated planning

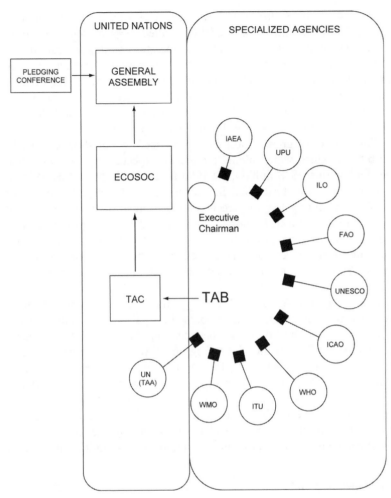

Figure 1.1 Structure of the Expanded Programme of Technical Assistance (EPTA)

within countries with the concept of a percentage allocation of funds to the specialized agencies."[10] It was agreed at ECOSOC that, from 1955, fixed shares would be ended, but to placate the agencies, they would receive not less than 85 percent of the previous year's allocation. This constraint was abolished only in 1961.

Owen helped to ensure the amplification of country views through the fielding of a growing number of TAB representatives.[11] There were three at the start of EPTA in 1950, but the number grew steadily to 15 in 1952, 45 in 1958, and over 70 when UNDP was created in the mid-1960s. From the mid-1950s, ECOSOC called for a loosening of automatic agency shares in favor of more deliberate "country programming." It was an important step toward releasing program formulation from procrustean sectoral apportionments, but in practice it did little to dampen the determination of the agencies to ensure they were present in every country allocation. These pressures were felt at the field level, where the TAB representatives became targets for agency advocacy.

Funding levels grew steadily, but continued to fall short of EPTA's ambitions, which were inflated by agency expectations. By 1955 pledges had risen to $28 million; by 1960 to $34 million; and by 1965 to $56 million, with the United States remaining the largest contributor by far, accounting for 40 percent of the total into the 1960s. Actual contributions fell a little short of pledges, and payments were delayed, but EPTA's funding problems were mainly the result of expectations running ahead of available resources, necessitating periodic retrenchments. Stop–go cycles have bedeviled UN system TA from the earliest stages.

A review in 1965 of EPTA's 15 years as an independent entity revealed that the program had disbursed a total of $457 million in 150 countries, with one third of the spending in Asia. Four agencies accounted for 77 percent of the program: FAO (24 percent), UN (21), WHO (17), and UNESCO (15). Nearly three-quarters of the programmed funds (net of administrative costs) went on expert services, and the next largest share was for 31,000 fellowships awarded during that period.[12] The EPTA was certainly ubiquitous, but its services were spread very thinly. It was one of the reasons why the UN sought to establish a complementary facility to support larger, multi-year projects.

The Special Fund

The Special Fund came into being nine years after EPTA, but it had much longer antecedents and it had been conceived on a much larger scale than EPTA. One of the most prominent campaigners for a UN role in development finance was the first person David Owen had asked to join him in the secretariat following his own appointment in 1946. Hans Singer was one of the early "brains" in the UN: a reputed academic,[13] as well as a fount of sound ideas and proposals. Singer wrote a paper for Owen on "pre-investment," which led to a proposal for a Special UN Fund for Economic Development (SUNFED). SUNFED would have created a single large capital investment fund supporting development projects through grants and soft loans, and it must have been part of the inspiration for Jackson's 1959 proposal for an International Development Authority (IDA). Debate on the proposal ebbed and flowed almost throughout the 1950s, with the developing countries in support and the United States and United Kingdom against. Its critics were doubtful about the wisdom of a fund governed by the General Assembly, in which the main contributors could be outvoted.[14] A satisfactory form of governance under UN auspices could certainly have been found, but the two most prominent banking nations took a conservative line, which drew them more naturally to an organization that they could control through voting shares: the International Bank for Reconstruction and Development (World Bank).[15] There was some irony in the fact that Owen, Singer, and others in the UN had been exhorting the World Bank to commence soft lending to developing countries, against the stolid resistance of Eugene Black, its President throughout this period.

As so often with his ideas, Singer's prescience prevailed, although not in the manner he had anticipated, and he had had in the meantime to suffer vilification by Republicans in the US Congress.[16] In 1958, ECOSOC and the General Assembly had authorized the creation of a Special Fund of the UN, but with functions complementary to the TA activities of the system. In the words of General Assembly resolution 1240, the Fund "would be directed towards enlarging the scope of the UN programmes of TA so as to include special projects in certain basic fields."[17] The following year, the World Bank agreed to establish the curiously-named International Development Association specifically for the purpose of extending concessional loans to developing countries. It was not Robert Jackson's International Development Authority, but it had many of the same objectives as SUNFED. The World Bank's IDA was to be funded from donor contributions ("replenishments") on a triennial basis, augmented by profits from the Bank's other operations. The new IDA confirmed the readiness of the donor community to set up a major new funding facility within the multilateral system, but the World Bank had won the main prize while the Special Fund was seen by many as a sop for the UN. While Singer's concerns about meeting the financial needs of developing countries through soft lending had been met, the advent of the new IDA helped to establish the World Bank—although formally a "UN specialized agency"—as a major development cooperation rival of the UN development system.

The same authorizing resolution of the General Assembly spelt out the guiding principles and criteria of the Special Fund. The "basic fields" would include mining, manufacturing, infrastructure, health, statistics, and public administration. It would finance "relatively large projects [...] with the widest possible impact [...] in particular by facilitating new capital investment." The latter reference opened the door to pre-investment studies, a throwback to earlier UN proposals, and in this respect the Special Fund came to complement the World Bank's own lending program under the IDA.

The Special Fund brought two more giants of the postwar development era into the UN spotlight. Paul Hoffman, who had successfully managed the Marshall Plan, became the head of the Special Fund, eschewing the designated title managing director in favor of Administrator—as he had been known at the Plan. His deputy was the redoubtable Arthur Lewis from St Lucia, a pioneer of development theory who was to become a Nobel laureate in economics in 1979. In an enlightened early decision, Hoffman sought to maintain cooperation among the big three funding entities by naming the UN Secretary-General Dag Hammarskjöld, Eugene Black, and David Owen to his Consultative Board.

At the Fund, Hoffman saw his job as raising money and Lewis's as spending it,[18] although in practice that task fell to Myer Cohen, head of programming. The first pledges to the Special Fund amounted to $26 million, which fell far short of the requests for assistance during the first year of $160 million. However, contributions grew quickly, and by 1966 the level had risen to almost $100 million. During the first five years of the Fund, 421 projects had been implemented in 130 countries with a total cost to the Fund of $374 million. These funds, however, were merely the core since the beneficiary countries themselves contributed $545 million to the same projects, many of which led to further domestic and foreign investments, especially in infrastructure.[19]

ECOSOC designated a Governing Council to oversee operations of the Fund, which was also advised by Hoffman's consultative board. Most projects were executed by the UN specialized agencies, but some were also contracted out to private companies. There were no formal agency shares, as in EPTA, but much maneuvering for advantage, both in New York, where final decisions were taken on projects, and in developing countries, where the resident representatives also assumed roles on behalf of the Fund.

A number of criteria guided the approval of Fund projects. They were intended to be larger than those of EPTA and spread over several years, but—in the case of institutional support—with a clear cut-off date to encourage sustainability. Projects were to fall within a coherent economic policy framework and lead to tangible outcomes, although it is not clear what specific methodology was applied to determine these.

OPEX and the principles of partnership

The formative years of UN TA were a period of experimentation. Underlying the process of bringing new institutions and programs to life there was alternation between two approaches to the relationships between developed and "underdeveloped" countries: one was based on a philosophy of aid as a form of patronage, and the other was based on the principles of partnership. The distinctions between the two approaches were often obscured by language. Over time, the expression "development cooperation" came to be preferred to aid. Technical assistance became technical cooperation; recipients became partners. But, notwithstanding growing preoccupations with developing country ownership of the development process, the change was essentially semantic. By the time the 1960s arrived, the trend had been in exactly the opposite direction. Aid—and TA in particular—had veered strongly toward patronage. The reasons were not hard to determine. The aid industry had multiplied in size, with major new bilateral programs leading the way, presenting developing countries with a wide array of essentially free TA to supplement multilateral sources. Bilateral aid was almost invariably an adjunct of donor foreign policy and bought influence.[20] But aid from one source had to compete with other offers. In these competitive circumstances, it was inevitable that UN assistance should also come to resemble patronage.

And there was another reason, which had more to do with the entitlement system built into UN TA, and which reinforced supply-sidedness. Hugh Keenleyside, one of the pioneers of UN assistance and a conscientious chronicler of the early years, succinctly described the phenomenon in a single sentence:

> Within a year after the Expanded Programme began, it sometimes seemed that the chief reason for undertaking a particular project was not the fact that the applicant government had placed it high on its list of priorities, but merely that a particular agency had money available and was willing to finance it."[21]

"Sometimes" was to become more and more habitual: developing countries would be assisted almost without asking.

Yet many in the UN were wedded to a philosophy of partnership and had sought to introduce cooperative elements into its programming. The principles were founded on funding: a requesting country was more likely to receive pertinent advice and support if it involved some financial obligation. Hoffman (for whom the term aid was anathema) brought to the Special Fund some of the principles of the quintessentially cooperative Marshall Plan, and the Fund's projects usually required substantial counterpart resources from partner governments, as the record shows. As early as 1950, a "Bolivian Plan" for a similar program of cooperation was mooted following an EPTA mission there (led by Keenleyside). It was designed to provide "operational and executive personnel" (OPEX) to developing countries. But OPEX personnel were not experts in the usual sense. They were provided through the UN, but recruited into public service by requesting countries, which paid them local salaries. These were topped up by the UN, but on a strictly time-limited basis, since the foreign personnel were expected to identify and train their own replacements within a one- or two-year period. In 1956, Dag Hammarskjöld himself took up the call for OPEX, which he envisaged as a fully fledged "international administrative service." The proposal ran into opposition when it came up for discussion in ECOSOC. Rather disingenuously, some of the former colonial powers—prime practitioners of aid as influence—accused the UN of wanting to control the policies of the developing countries through OPEX, whereas the scheme was designed specifically to ensure control lay with the hosts.[22] OPEX was afforded a cautious start in 1959 with a modest allocation, which funded 11 positions in the first year. By 1961, after a successful two years of operation and with many requests outstanding, the program was given more permanent status within the UN and grew steadily.

Another partnership scheme was called "Funds in Trust," or, in alternative UN jargon, TA on a "payments basis". Under this scheme, developing countries could obtain additional services to those received under EPTA by paying the increments themselves in hard currency, for example to extend the services of a foreign expert or in other ways prolong the life of a project. By 1965, no fewer than 64 countries had purchased services from the UN through this means, seeming to belie any presumption that foreign advisory services were unaffordable.[23]

But perhaps the most significant *démarche* in fostering partnership was the successful effort, led by David Owen, to persuade developing countries to sign "Standard Basic Assistance Agreements" (SBAA) with the UN TAB. The resolution creating EPTA had fallen short of prescribing the nature and amounts of counterpart resources, but governments requesting assistance "were expected to agree [...] normally to assume responsibility for a substantial part of the costs of technical services with which they are provided, at least that part which can be paid in their own currencies." Owen's agreements went much further. Developing countries were to defray the costs of local personnel and of the transportation, communications, and medical services of all program staff. Countries were expected to provide office accommodation to resident representatives, and contributions were to be made to local allowances of experts, including all local taxes. Each government was also required to pay cash amounts of "local counterpart costs" and to uphold the diplomatic privileges and immunities of international personnel. Over the period 1950–64, during which donor countries pledged $400 million for EPTA, hard-currency contributions from developing countries amounted to $45 million. Much more significant, however, was an estimated $900 million in local costs borne by the beneficiaries.[24] To enforce the agreements, the TAB would refuse additional requests for assistance to countries in arrears.

But the agreements began to unravel from the early stages. Developing countries perceived the incongruity between agency entitlement and recipient obligation, and TAB resident representatives came under pressure to soften or waive the conditions of the SBAAs. No later than 1951, the executive boards of UNESCO and WHO passed resolutions absolving governments from paying all prescribed costs for their own experts. It was one of many examples of Dutch auctioning in an increasingly competitive development system.

The birth of UNDP

During the 1960s, creative minds among the governments and civil servants of the UN system had brought to life a growing number of instruments for dispensing TA. They included the regular budget programs of TA from the UN and the specialized agencies: a total of ten different sources. During the 1950s, EPTA was the principal source of TA for the UN and most of the specialized agencies, supplemented by OPEX and Funds in Trust arrangements. Then, at the end of the decade, came the Special Fund with projections of an even larger scale of resources.

By the beginning of the 1960s, EPTA and the Special Fund were following different programming practices: the former moving toward more decentralization, while the Fund kept formulation and approval in New York. Given the related nature of their businesses, there was a strong case for closer alignment, and in 1961 a committee to study a possible merger was established with members drawn from the EPTA's TAC and the Fund's Governing Council. In a 1962 General Assembly resolution (1768), the TAC was asked to go further in proposing a rationalization of programs, including those funded from regular budgets.[25] There were arguments on both sides—sometimes within the same governments.[26] While foreign ministries might favor merger, line ministries did not always toe the same line when speaking in the governing bodies of the specialized agencies. Following two years of deliberation, at the beginning of 1964 the Secretary-General put forward a proposal for merger, but he excluded the regular programs. The merger was agreed by ECOSOC and the General Assembly in the same year,[27] to take effect the following January. So, in 1965, Hoffman—representing the largest donor—became UNDP's first Administrator, and Owen his deputy, or co-administrator.

The birth of UNDP was a minor triumph of UN rationalization. It also carried the prospect of substantial grant resources becoming available to the UN system, both for a wide range of technical support services and for the identification of investment projects through feasibility studies, which would have cemented the relationship with the World Bank (and later the regional development banks). In practice, following the merger, the identity of the two funds was gradually lost and the pre-investment role of UNDP disappeared.

Organizationally, the new UNDP also carried deficient genes, which inhibited the creation of a strong and cohesive UN development system. In the first place, the funding relationship with the agencies was fraught. At the birth of UNDP, the specialized agencies were locked into a system of automatic TA "patronage." While WHO and the International Atomic Energy Agency (IAEA) already had significant parallel TA programs financed by their regular budgets (not subject to any UN-wide coordination), they and the other specialized agencies also received allocations of funding from UNDP, which were protected jealously by their respective managements and administered separately, albeit with some oversight by UNDP's country representatives. To achieve real system-wide coherence would have required a mechanism that fully encompassed all the TA resources of the UN, but, by the time of UNDP's creation, this would have been unrealizable. As Chapter 2 reveals, however, UNDP was later to move in exactly the opposite direction.

A second potential fault-line was the voluntary nature of UNDP's funding. It began life as the principal source of UN TA, but every year it held pledging conferences to exhort maximum contributions from its main donors, which were relatively few. In good times, pledges might be unexpectedly high, but, because donors had their own domestic fiscal preoccupations, UNDP was also highly vulnerable to sudden falls in their contributions. Stop-and-go funding proved to be the pattern, and the volatility in UNDP's financial position undermined its status as a funding partner. Within ten years, UNDP would encounter its first full-blooded funding crisis.

Thirdly, while UNDP was an improved mechanism for administering UN TA, it began life—and has remained—more of a fund than a "program." What it lacked, and what could have made it a powerful program overseer, was a globally recognized development specialist as its head. There was unfortunately no pedigree for this. In the early days of UN TA, the UN Secretary-General could have appointed as its head Raúl Prebisch, or another person of similar intellectual caliber. In the event, a person was chosen from within the diplomatic entourage, a pattern that has been followed in senior UN appointments ever since. For UNDP's historian, the appointment "meant rejecting the principle that the UN development chief should be one of the most respected economists from the developing world."[28] It is true that some important "brains" have worked for, and been associated with, the UN and UNDP. Hans Singer and V. K. R. V. Rao, both students of Maynard Keynes, were active as UN economists from the 1940s onwards. UNDP also had two renowned international economists working as its deputies in the early days: W. Arthur Lewis, the first Nobel laureate in economics from outside the United States and Europe, and I.G. Patel, a renowned Indian economist. But, while it succeeded in attracting talented development specialists for specific task, UNDP has always been headed by an Administrator, chosen more for the skills associated with that title, including a capacity to raise funds from the major donors. In a system with a strict hierarchy and degree of atomization like the UN, it would have needed a development specialist of global renown as deputy Secretary-General for UNDP to have been regarded as the central "brain" of the development system. Repeated attempts to install a "director general" for development in the UN have acknowledged the need, but have not led to filling this important gap.

But, in the absence of a single cohesive UN development system, perhaps the greatest organizational paradox UNDP was to face was in trying to be both a "fund" and a "program." If it was really to take on more of the "brain" functions in UN programming, would it have wanted to stay wedded to the agencies as its exclusive partners and sole beneficiaries of its funding?

In the fourth place, the governance of the UN system, and the heterogeneity of its structure, has guaranteed a proliferation of programs and funding mechanisms. The fusion of EPTA and the Special Fund led to a welcome process of reconsolidation, but it did little to bring the specialized agencies into closer alignment. It would soon become clear that, with the structure that prevailed in the 1960s, the only alternative to full integration was disintegration. Over the long term, strong centrifugal forces were to drive the system further apart. But not before there had been an ambitious attempt to refashion the architecture soon after UNDP's creation.

The Capacity Study

At the instigation of another Democratic US President—John Kennedy—the 1960s were dubbed the United Nations Decade of Development. The development agenda was still being set in and around the UN, with inspiration coming from Raúl Prebisch, Arthur Lewis, Hans Singer, Nicholas Kaldor, and others. It was also the decade in which several key UN institutions were put in place, besides UNDP. Prebisch moved from the influential UN Economic Commission for Latin America (ECLA) to become the first Secretary-General of the UN Conference on Trade and Development (UNCTAD) established in 1964 in Geneva. The previous year had seen the creation of the World Food Programme (WFP) in Rome, and in 1969 the UN Population Fund (UNFPA) was set up in New York. Meanwhile in Washington, the World Bank—under the dynamic leadership of Robert McNamara—was growing in size and prominence, expanding its lending operations to the newly independent developing countries on the back of its own concessional finance arm, the IDA.

Toward the end of the decade, it was a time for stocktaking in order to align the roles and functions of this constellation of development institutions, UN and World Bank included. In 1968, two major commissions were established, one under the auspices of the World Bank, and the other at the behest of UNDP. The former was the Pearson Commission,[29] led by the former Canadian prime minister, and the latter was *A Study of the Capacity of the United Nations Development System* (hereafter the Capacity Study), which often carries the name of the commissioner, Robert Jackson.[30]

In the spring of 1968, UNDP's administrator, Paul Hoffman, approached Jackson to undertake a major study on the reform of the "UN development system." Jackson was a known reformer, having outlined his proposals for an International Development Authority in a set of lectures in 1959. This IDA would bring together all the UN programs of TA, combined with a soft loan facility, and coordinate assistance to developing countries on the basis of their own national programs. The UN specialized agencies would act as research centers and promoters of standards in their own fields, leaving TA to the IDA.[31] His "UN system" included the World Bank, and he saw UN grants and Bank loans as complementary. In practice, the UN agencies and the World Bank have become more competitive than collaborative over the years.

Hoffman recognized that the family of organizations at that date had grown by accretion from diverse origins, describing it as a "jungle of proliferating agencies."[32] If the UN was to have anything resembling a coherent development system, then it required a proper blueprint. Jackson was initially reluctant to undertake the study—perhaps because he was doubtful of the outcome—but he agreed to become Commissioner when his choice of Joan Anstee as his main collaborator ("Chief of Staff") was accepted. The study thus brought together two of the most accomplished field operations specialists in the UN's history. Anstee herself had headed UN field missions for 15 years in different regions, and was well-placed to judge the effectiveness of the development system. A radical report was presaged by the fact that she was already (in her own words) "one of the system's most vociferous critics."[33]

From the Geneva area, the two worked with a small team intensively for most of 1969, finishing the report at the end of September, in time to be submitted in the six UN languages to official delegations prior to debate in the January 1970 session of the UNDP Governing Council. It was a defining moment for the system, which, as the report acknowledged, had been flawed by its piecemeal creation. What the Capacity Study provided was an integrating solution. It was the first real opportunity to apply architecture to a UN development collectivity, without which it would continue to be a "system" in name only.

The Capacity Study[34] revived the notion of the IDA as an ideal model, but recognized that with the passing of time it had become difficult to overturn entrenched institutional practices. The most realistic aim was more coherence and alignment, and the study set out ten operating principles (or "precepts") as the basis for its proposals (see Box 1.1). Within this framework, the proposals were nevertheless far-reaching.

The TA operations of the agencies—financed mainly with UNDP money according to prescribed shares—had become the large tail wagging each of the dogs, and accounted for much of their growth. But, like most aid at that time, it was supply driven, with project proposals emanating from the creative minds of agency staff according to their own specialized proclivities. It was not cognizant of development cooperation from other sources—UN or non-UN—and was not closely attuned to developing country needs.[35] The Capacity Study sought to turn the process around and encourage countries to develop integrated programs within a defined multi-year financial framework known as an Indicative Planning Figure (IPF).[36] The funding would still be channeled

Box 1.1 The "ten precepts" of the Capacity Study

1   The introduction of a programming method which would enable all inputs from the UN development system to be programmed comprehensively at one time in a program corresponding to the needs and the duration of each country's national development plan.

2   Effective and prompt execution of approved projects, having recourse, as necessary, to all available methods and resources within and without the system.

3   Controlled evaluation, designed to maintain the accountability of the Administrator of UNDP for the use of all resources contributed to UNDP, to measure results, to judge the effectiveness of the methods used, and to draw conclusions which may be applied with benefit to future operations.

4   Effective follow-up conceived as an integral part of each project from the outset.

5   The introduction of an efficient information system.

6   Organizational reforms at the country, regional and head-quarters level designed to integrate the components of the UN development system more closely. These should combine greater control at the center with maximum decentralization to the field level, where the authority of the resident representative should be greatly strengthened.

7   Proper staffing of the operation at all levels, involving far-reaching measures to attract and retain the best qualified people available.

8   A financial framework designed to ensure the smooth running of the operation, through which the maximum possible amount of funds entrusted to the UN development system for development cooperation should be channeled, the head of the central organization being held personally accountable for their use.

9   Maximum use of all modern managerial and administrative aids and techniques to ensure an effective, expeditious and economical operation.

10 Maximum flexibility on the part of governments and the system alike to permit adaptability to changing circumstances and a speedy and effective response to new challenges and opportunities as they arise.

A Study of the Capacity of the UN Development System (Geneva:
United Nations, 1969), Volume I, para. 61.

to the agencies through UNDP, but pre-allocated to countries according to various development criteria, out of projected estimates of funds' availability. UNDP's in-country Resident Representatives would be responsible for managing each country program.

UNDP headquarters was to be reorganized so as to better serve the field, with the creation of four regional bureaux. Apart from overseeing their respective country offices, these regional bureaux were intended to work closely with the UN regional commissions, with the possibility of outposting the bureaux to the same locations. At headquarters, the specialized agencies would provide their own contributions to UNDP's substantive thinking through a Technical Advisory Panel. The Study also proposed the establishment of a Development Resources Panel comprising the heads of UNDP, World Bank, IMF,[37] UNCTAD, UNICEF, WFP, and the UN Department of Economic and Social Affairs (UN DESA) to "harmonize policies and integrate activities between UNDP and the other components of the UN system which are the principal providers of inputs or are responsible for general policies which influence the development process."[38]

The Capacity Study ran to over 500 pages and contained an impressive amount of analysis of the contemporary TA arrangements of the UN. There were also many recommendations of an administrative and managerial nature, including an "information systems concept" (Capacity Study, chapter 6 and precept number 5) designed to serve as a means of sharing and unifying knowledge within the system.

Jackson was pragmatic. He envisaged two phases for implementation of his recommendations over a period of five years. But his vision of the ideal model still shone through in the report through references to longer-term objectives. In a telling coda to the key chapter on organization (Capacity Study, chapter 7), he set out "the ultimate objective" for the system, which included the appointment of a director-general as supreme overseer, an integrated structure under the Economic and Social Council, centralized budgetary control for all entities, and the merger of the UNDP regional bureaux with the regional commissions.[39]

Although not as radical as it needed to be to create an effective development system, the study had a very mixed reception. It badly needed a champion in the system, but even Paul Hoffman was skeptical. He probably took umbrage at some of the language of the study, which followed Jackson's sometimes feisty and colorful style. Contemporaries of Hoffman believe that he was particularly offended by some of the words in the prefatory volume, which he misconstrued as criticism.[40] For example:

The UN development system has tried to wage a war on want for many years with very little organized "brain" to guide it. Its absence may well be the greatest constraint of all on capacity. Without it, the future evolution of the UN development system could easily repeat the history of the dinosaur.[41]

His lieutenants had other reasons to be hostile. Up to that point, UNDP derived a lot of its power from the centralized system of approving large projects and allocating resources, in which it exercised considerable discretion,[42] albeit contrary to the principles of multilateralism. As in all attempted reform processes, organizational inertia played its part in generating hostility in the rest of the system. In a dilution of the supply-driven nature of TA, the specialized agencies saw their cozy relationships with UNDP beginning to fray, as programming responsibilities were shifted to the field. Their recourse was to strengthen their ties with their counterpart ministries in the developing countries (FAO with ministries of agriculture, UNESCO with education, and so on) and encourage them to generate demands for TA.

The study was discussed in the regular UNDP Governing Council in January 1970, and again in March at a special session. Fortunately, the reception by the developing countries was much more positive, finding champions in Cuba, India, and Iran. Many of the key donor countries were also in favor of the reforms. The outcome was the so-called Consensus resolution approved by the Governing Council in June 1970, with further refinements at its session in January 1971.[43]

As its name suggests, and in the nature of all intergovernmental deliberations, the Consensus was a compromise: a watershed for some, but for others, including Joan Anstee, it was still "inherently defective."[44] It fell short of what the Capacity Study had considered feasible in the short term, but prescribed some changes to UNDP and the development system to correct what had become a rather centralized patronage mechanism. Country programming was endorsed, and with it a funding entitlement based on the IPF, determined by income per head and population size. But the programming frameworks were fixed at five years and were the same for all countries, rather than following local planning cycles. There were to be four new regional bureaux of UNDP (but with no anticipated merger with the regional commissions). More authority was to be given to resident representatives (renamed as resident directors, a term that did not stick). Their authority extended to UNDP funds and programs, but not to other agencies in the same country, as the Capacity Study had proposed.

The system is dead, long live the system …

The years 1969 and 1970 were two of the most fateful for UNDP and the UN development system. In the circumstances of the time—and in the absence of strong commitments to reform at the top of the UN—it was already too late to attempt the construction of the unified UN development system envisaged by Jackson's ideal model.[45] Then, and subsequently, it would have required a huge act of political will from within and outside the UN to forge a system capable of smoothly combining the best UN expertise to address the redoubtable development challenges for which a UN would have been uniquely qualified. The system still had no central "brain"—either in person or in function. It had a wide variety of norm-setting and regulatory functions, and a disjointed array of TA interventions, but no central policy console. Instead, there was an atomized network of cerebral functions residing in many different physical and organizational locations. A critical lacuna of the Consensus was the virtual omission of any consideration of the "information systems concept" to which the Capacity Study had devoted its longest chapter, and which could have underpinned the network. Instead, the system has been connected by increasingly elaborate mechanisms of coordination.

The preparation of the Capacity Study, and the Consensus that resulted, had the effect of halting any further realistic prospect of creating a unified development system similar to Jackson's IDA. Had such a system been created, the UN's weight in supporting the development process might have grown rather than diminished. For reasons that will become apparent as this story unfolds, the absence of UN coherence and the consequent—and growing—dispersion of resources opened a vacuum that was filled by the World Bank: a more tightly knit, well-managed, competent, and resource-rich organization. Its ascendancy guaranteed the prevalence of a conservative western development paradigm and the application of banking strictures to the unpredictable and idiosyncratic contexts of development. In many ways, the dominance of the Bank made a UN alternative even more important, even as the UN's influence waned.

New dimensions for UNDP

Through the Capacity Study and the ensuing Consensus, however, Jackson helped to create a more viable UNDP, even if he had not succeeded with his larger blueprint. The Consensus ushered in some needed internal reforms and clarified the relationship of UNDP with the agencies. It was the beginning, not the end, of a process of rein-vention and adjustment that has been a characteristic of UNDP throughout its existence.

The next set of reforms followed shortly afterwards, when a new management was installed. In 1969, Owen left UNDP, and in 1972, Hoffman—already in his eighties—retired. The United States was contributing about 40 percent of UNDP's funds and, as with the World Bank (and UNICEF), it was considered the prerogative of the White House to choose the UNDP Administrator. President Nixon nominated Rudolph Peterson who, pledging to double the US con-tribution, was duly confirmed by the Governing Council. Peterson was another outsider, a prominent banker who had previously advised Nixon on international development. While Administrator, he con-tinued his advisory functions at the Bank of America in California. Partly in consequence, he took time to establish his new management team, but made two excellent choices in appointing his two deputies: I. G. Patel of India (for programs) and Bert Lindstrom of Sweden (administration).

Patel was something of a square peg. Although he had worked in his government, as well as the IMF (and as alternate Executive Director of the World Bank), he found UNDP to be without substance, exces-sively bureaucratic, and process-oriented.[46] Even the Bretton Woods institutions were more nimble. He felt that UNDP TA was too cir-cumscribed by rules and restrictions, and set out to bring in more flexibility with a proposal called "New Dimensions in Technical Coop-eration," approved by the General Assembly in December 1975.[47] In an important sense, "New Dimensions" took the country ownership principles of the Capacity Study a step further, providing for "govern-ment execution" of projects. This also meant widening the choices of implementation arrangements, including through the use of national (as opposed to exclusively UN international) experts. Patel was at odds with some of the traditionalists in UNDP, who saw the organization's primary role as an anchor to the development system and an exclusive user of UN expertise. But if UNDP was to shift more programming initiative to its client countries, it would seem natural for them to require a wider choice of implementing partners, including those outside the UN.

There were at least three reasons for UNDP's inclination to diversify. One was frustration at the uneven performance of the UN agencies. Some of this frustration may have been disingenuous, since UNDP was responsible for helping governments choose UN projects and for over-seeing their implementation. But there was little doubt that many projects fell short of their objectives, especially in countries where UN agencies had no permanent presence and managed their operations remotely.

A second reason was that UN agencies did not always have the requisite expertise to offer. The UN development system was a finite set of organizations and agencies with specific mandates, for the most part mirroring the public sectors of developing countries. Expertise in such areas as management, entrepreneurship, or marketing fell outside the purview of the system and had to be sought elsewhere.

A third reason was the sluggishness of the project implementation process itself. Just identifying and approving projects on a three-cornered basis (government/UNDP/agency) was cumbersome, and three bureaucracies again had to be traversed for approval and agreement on the implementation arrangements. In UNDP's early years also, project spending ("delivery") was low even after approval. This displeased the donors, and the United States in particular. Using government execution, these processes could be short-circuited.

A seemingly natural, but for the development system symbolically fateful, step taken by the Peterson administration was the establishment in UNDP of the Office of Project Execution. The OPE (later to be renamed the UN Office for Project Services, UNOPS) was an in-house facility and enabled UNDP to organize its own implementation arrangements expeditiously, commissioning and fielding experts and services from non-UN sources. Coupled with "government execution," the use of OPE effectively meant UNDP implementing projects on behalf of client countries. They appreciated the greater speed and flexibility. For UNDP, it was a step in the direction of becoming more "program" than "fund," while also more autonomous within the development system. But OPE was like a red rag to the agencies, which had become accustomed to the cozy entitlement relationship with UNDP.[48] Although OPE was intended to be used only outside the agencies' fields of expertise, the new entity directly reduced the funding available to the traditional partners while sending a clear message that there was now a direct competitor in the pen. OPE/UNOPS has enjoyed checkered fortunes since, but in recent years it has re-emerged as a very effective facility. It operates on a quasi-commercial basis, performing services in project management, procurement, and human and financial resources management in several specific fields. It derives all its revenue from commissions, which are increasingly from outside UNDP and the UN system, including from governments (which in 2009 accounted for over a quarter of its revenues). UNOPS has thus become an example of a demand-driven UN organization.

In mid-1975, UNDP ran into a full-blown funding crisis, mainly of its own making. Voluntary funding can entail increases as well as reductions and in that year—despite an overall increase in pledges— two donors fell well short. UNDP had been counting on receiving arrears of $16 million from the Italian government, and pledges of $90 million and $100 million from the United States in 1974 and 1975. But the arrears were not paid and the US shortfall was more than $40 million. Expenditures in 1975 also jumped to over $500 million, a sharp increase on the previous year, mainly as a result of much larger obligations incurred by the UN agencies. These were imponderables. However, there is little doubt that UNDP went headlong into the crisis without allowing for worst-case contingencies. Records at the time reveal that the expected financial position had to be revised downwards several times during 1975.[49]

In fact, from 1973 onwards, total voluntary pledges to UNDP increased significantly each year of the decade. The crisis was therefore largely an artificial one, created by over-optimistic projections of revenue and poor control over expenditures. The repercussions of this first fully fledged funding crisis were unfortunate for both UNDP and the system. Many projects had to be curtailed (or "leveled off," as the Governing Council was politely informed) and considerable uncertainty was sown in the agencies and, more importantly, in beneficiary countries. The crisis revealed the potential pitfalls of trying to develop five-year program frameworks containing multi-year projects on the basis on voluntary annual funding replenishments.

New programs

Because TA has been offered almost free of charge in the postwar period, purveyors of aid have been motivated by the need to maximize resources. Since these resources have come almost exclusively from a limited number of richer donor countries, it has been their agendas, as much as those of the developing countries, that have influenced the content of programs. It has not been different in the UN system, except that "multilateralism" has helped to ensure that all member states are eligible to receive assistance (as opposed to the greater selectivity of bilateral aid).[50]

UNDP, whose original *raison d'être* was based on mobilizing funds, has always been good at taking advantage of the willingness of donors to fund new programs, and even whole organizations. These specific funding opportunities have helped to broaden the base of its support, even if it has not always managed to sustain overall resource levels.

The impact on the development system has been to influence its structure in favor of the development interests of donors, even when the interests of developing countries have not been strongly manifested.

An example was the creation in 1969 of the UN Fund for Population Activities (UNFPA), an organization with fund-pulling potential that "could actively pursue the population side of development at a time when many African, Asian and Latin American governments considered the issue to be a diversion [...]."[51] The idea had originally been Paul Hoffman's, who first incubated the population program within UNDP. He had brought Rafael Salas from the Philippines to raise funds and run it, both of which he accomplished with great success, remaining as the Executive Director of UNFPA for its first 18 years. During his tenure, and that of his successor Nafis Sadik, UNFPA (which became known as the UN Population Fund) widened its brief from an early focus on population control and helped to consolidate support in the developing world. Today, the organization's work encompasses population planning, reproductive health, HIV/AIDS prevention, and women's empowerment.

The difficulties of donor supply-sidedness were to manifest themselves much later, however. UNFPA fell foul of a strong anti-abortion lobby in the US Congress, which succeeded in stopping all US contributions in 2002. The freeze was lifted only in 2009, and over the seven years the organization had accumulated a shortfall of $250 million from the United States alone. UNFPA had been forced to curtail its activities when the need for its services was growing.

Several other programs and organizations were started in the early years of UNDP. One year after the merger, the General Assembly approved the creation of the UN Capital Development Fund (UNCDF), which in 1971 was given to UNDP to manage. The "capital" referred to resources for the purchase of equipment, designed to supplement UNDP's TA projects in the least-developed countries. UNCDF never saw a significant expansion in its funding, and there were periodic discussions about folding it fully into UNDP. But it was kept afloat with support from a few European donors. In more recent years, it has come to specialize in supporting micro-finance, receiving its largest contribution from the private Bill & Melinda Gates Foundation.[52]

In 1971, the UN Volunteers program was started, initially with funding from Iran. Its early funding prospects were poor, but after a few years the traditional donors were mobilized, and the program has enjoyed steady growth over 40 years. UNVs are mostly well-trained professionals in specialized fields from developing countries. As volunteers they receive a stipend rather than a full salary, serve for one or a few years only, and are not expected to move on to careers in the UN system (although some do). UNV has been a success story for UNDP. Apart from providing cost-effective TA and mobilizing expertise quickly and flexibly, it has played exactly the kind of servicing role within the UN system originally envisaged for UNDP. Today, some two-thirds of UNVs work in the projects of other UN agencies.[53]

With an initial grant from the Netherlands, UNDP also set up a trust fund in 1973 for national liberation movements. Although bilateral funding from some (e.g. Nordic and East European) governments was already being channeled to these movements,[54] the creation of a UN trust fund was an enlightened move, immediately giving more universal legitimacy to the cause of independence. UNDP earmarked program funds (IPFs) for several countries to be spent by the respective liberation movements. The targets of assistance were in Africa, particularly those movements mobilized against white minority rule in South Africa and Zimbabwe (African National Council) and Namibia (South-West African People's Organization), as well as against the Portuguese colonies. Although the amounts of funding were modest, UNDP gained considerable credence with the governments of those countries when they gained their independence. The trust fund also set an important UN precedent of intervention. Post-independence, it was replaced by the virtually sacrosanct principle of sovereignty. But the principle of internal intervention was revived in 1992, when the UN invoked Chapter VII of the Charter for its military operations in Somalia,[55] and has returned with the debate on the "responsibility to protect," enshrined in the Outcome Document of the World Summit in 2005.[56]

Other funds were set up for specific purposes. The UN Revolving Fund for Natural Resources Exploration was aimed at mobilizing support from oil-exporting countries, which had benefited from the huge price increases after 1973, in order to further mineral exploration in poorer countries. As the name suggests, the fund extended credits and was intended to be replenished from the eventual production of new discoveries. The UN Financing System for Science and Technology for Development (UNFSSTD) and the UN Special Fund for Land-locked Developing Countries were other examples of special-purpose funds. These funding facilities also relied on limited numbers of donors. The UNFSSTD provided for separate trust funds to be set up under its auspices to allow a particular donor to support a particular project (an example being Italian funding of a rural technology project in Indonesia in 1983). In the strict sense, therefore, this was not multilateral assistance.

The golden partnership

Peterson's term was short-lived, and he left in the year of the funding crisis. He was replaced in 1976 by the other most senior American then serving in the UN, Bradford Morse, Under-Secretary-General for Political Affairs since 1972. A former Republican congressman, Morse was to remain for the longest period of any Administrator: ten years. As before, Nixon made the nomination and, despite the record of his predecessor, it was assumed that he would help to sustain US contributions to UNDP.

In 1978, he appointed Arthur Brown from Jamaica as his sole Deputy, following the departure of both Patel and Lindstrom. It was an outstanding choice. Morse was good at rousing morale and keeping UNDP in the public eye. He also helped to turn around the funding situation, but not in the way anticipated. Brown, who came to UNDP via the Jamaican central bank and the International Bauxite Association, was well attuned to the needs of the developing countries. Morse was "fund" to Brown's "program" and, although very different in character, they were sufficiently complementary that each had his own distinct field of interest. It was a very productive partnership.

Between 1970 and 1980, total funding almost tripled in current US dollar terms to $692 million (although the increase was much smaller in real terms). However, the pattern of patronage changed in one fundamental way. Support for the UN from the US administration and Congress was weakening, and never again recovered the dominant role it had exercised from Truman's time. There was concern over the strident demands from developing countries within the UN for a "new international economic order." The US was also preoccupied with an unpopular and expensive war in Vietnam.[57] However, as US contributions fell away, Morse was successful in persuading the northern Europeans to increase their funding. In 1970, the United States still contributed 38 percent of UNDP's resources, but ten years later this had declined to 18 percent. Over the same period, the combined proportion accounted by Sweden, Denmark, Norway, and the Netherlands rose from 23 to 38 percent—an interesting reversal.[58] From then onwards, the real (and even current) value of the US's contributions declined, while the contributions of the four Europeans was well sustained.

During Morse's tenure, UNDP was still important to the UN development family. The improved funding situation made UNDP a stronger partner for the agencies, even if their total share was declining. But the centrality of UNDP's position had diminished—in 1981 UNDP accounted for only 11 percent of the total development expenditures of the UN system[59]—and it was at risk from other legislative developments. In 1975, the General Assembly had set up an *ad hoc* Committee on the Restructuring of the Economic and Social Sectors of the United Nations System, which reported to the General Assembly. At the end of 1977, the General Assembly passed a comprehensive resolution based on the committee's report.[60] The committee and the General Assembly resolution were part of another attempt to forge a greater measure of coherence in the UN development system, but again the outcome was less than the aspiration.

There were several features of relevance to the organizational relationship of UNDP to the rest of the system. The most significant proposal was the designation of a post of Director-General for Development and International Economic Cooperation (DG), to be appointed by the Secretary-General, whose tasks would be:

> Ensuring the provision of effective leadership to the various components of the United Nations system in the field of development and international economic cooperation and in exercising overall coordination within the system in order to ensure a multi-disciplinary approach to the problems of development on a system-wide basis; ensuring, within the United Nations, the coherence, coordination and efficient management of all activities in the economic and social fields financed by the regular budget or by extra-budgetary resources.[61]

On paper, this was a promising step towards integration in the system, the need for which had been identified 25 years earlier. However, the proposal was compromised by one critical detail: the level of the post. Developing country members of the *ad hoc* Committee had proposed that the new DG should occupy a post "corresponding to a level higher than that of under-secretary-general."[62] With this proposal, the DG would then have been the most senior person in the entire UN system, after the Secretary-General himself, giving the incumbent seniority over all the heads of specialized agencies. This move would have been strongly resisted by the agencies—management and governors—and the final wording of the resolution merely established the level as "commensurate with the functions" of the post. In the event, a Ghanaian diplomat was appointed as the first DG in 1978 at the level of under-secretary-general.[63] The choice was less than ideal,[64] and the post proved to be largely ineffective in terms of leading the UN development system. In 1982, the second and last DG was appointed for another four-year term, after which the post lapsed.

A strong DG would also have caused some discomfort for UNDP, since it effectively switched leadership of the development system to the Secretary-General and the UN secretariat. More significant for the organization was the resolution's proposal to strengthen system coordination at country level by designating a single official with "overall responsibility for, and coordination of, operational activities for development."[65] These positions were later to be designated as UN resident coordinators (for operational activities for development) and, although the resolution had specified that appointments would be made "taking into account the sectors of particular interest to the countries of assignment," the positions were almost invariably given to the sitting UNDP resident representatives. There was expediency in giving the country coordination role to UNDP. But creating two functions for the UNDP representative led to ambiguities, and did nothing to dampen inter-agency rivalries. If, at the outset, a wholly separate senior post for overseeing the UN development system in each country had been created, the system might have achieved a degree of development coherence, at least at that level.

Two other features of the resolution are worth noting. One was the renewed attempt to establish the primacy of ECOSOC in deliberating on development issues and recommending policy guidelines for operational activities. It is a measure of the feeble impact of this resolution that comprehensive new reviews of ECOSOC's functioning have been proposed almost every year up to the present.

The resolution also attempted to give more meaningful roles to the five UN regional commissions, by designating them as the "main general economic and social development centres within the UN system." The regional commissions were well placed to act as hubs for regional cooperation among developing countries, and being designated subsequently as executing agencies for UNDP funding gave them an operational dimension. The resolution was careful to condition the roles of the regional commissions with respect to the rest of the system "having due regard to the responsibilities of the specialized agencies and other United Nations bodies in specific sectoral fields and the coordinating role of UNDP." But in practice, the regional commissions—which were to become executing agencies in 1979—began to take on a range of operational functions that went beyond their mandates of inter-country cooperation. As regional microcosms of the system, they began undertaking country projects in parallel with UNDP and the agencies. Unfortunately, there has never been any clear resolution of the division of labor between the global and regional UN in operational terms,[66] and General Assembly resolution 32/197 did not help to find it.

The 1970s unfolded against the background of a turbulent development debate in the UN on a "new international economic order" (NIEO). With the developing countries having a large majority in the main organs of the UN, the NIEO was an attempt to create more equitable global economic conditions. UNDP was not a part of the debate, except vicariously through its TA support of UN organizations such as UNCTAD, but both Morse and Brown were known to be sympathetic to the aims of the NIEO. What UNDP was nevertheless setting out to prove was that it could be the UN organization closest to the needs of developing countries, with its network of country offices, now headed by UN resident coordinators, officially appointed by the UN Secretary-General.

Bradford Morse also brought into UNDP a stronger humanitarian focus. In the early 1970s, western African countries of the Sahel had suffered a severe drought, leading to acute food shortages. The Secretary-General had established a Special Sahelian Office in the secretariat, and Morse was asked to head it, concurrently with his other responsibilities. The Office successfully mobilized much of its funding from oil-exporting countries, their revenues boosted by large increases in oil prices during the decade. When he joined UNDP, the Office—now called the UN Sahelian Office (UNSO)—came with him. While UNSO had been a secretariat body, the UNDP resident representatives in West Africa had shown limited interest in it,[67] but their attitude changed once it became part of their organization.

Another innovation during Morse's term was a program called "Transfer of Knowledge Through Expatriate Nationals" (TOKTEN). From the earliest stages, EPTA and UNDP had been generous in providing fellowships to developing countries to allow their nationals to study abroad for short or long periods. For many countries, the prospect of foreign training was one of the most attractive features of UN assistance. Fellowships, however, were not always managed very strategically. Not all local offices systematically screened applicants for their eligibility, nor did they put measures in place to ensure that fellows made the best use of their training once they returned. In some countries, many did not return at all,[68] and UNDP was sometimes criticized for contributing to the "brain drain" from the South. TOKTEN was a "brain gain." It provided skilled members of a country's diaspora with incentive payments to return home and act as advisers, or even to take on more permanent jobs. The progam has been managed by UNV, as TOKTEN consultants forgo professional fees and are paid travel costs and a daily allowance. The receiving institutions can be in the public or private sector. The program has

Box 1.2 The UNDP Administrators

1950–64 David Owen (United Kingdom), Executive Chairman, UN Technical Assistance Board

1965–69 Co-administrator, UNDP

David Owen's early career was spent at the University of Glasgow, where he was a lecturer. In 1946, he was the first person to be recruited to the UN secretariat in New York, where he became Assistant Secretary-General in charge of economic affairs. His most notable achievement was to bring the UN's EPTA into operation and to establish a network of resident representatives with responsibility for overseeing and managing TA at the country level. He was Executive Secretary and then Executive Chairman of the UN Technical Assistance Board until 1965, when EPTA was merged with the Special Fund to form UNDP. In 1965, he became Co-Administrator of UNDP, leaving the UN in 1969 to head the International Planned Parenthood Federation.

1959–64 Paul G. Hoffman (United States), Executive Director, UN Special Fund

1965–72 Administrator, UNDP

Paul Hoffman left college early to go into business, making his first million dollars as a salesman for Studebaker cars when still in his early thirties. Ten years later, he became president of Studebaker, helping to rescue the company from near-insolvency in the 1930s. In 1948, he was asked by President Harry Truman to head the Economic Cooperation Agency, the body administering the Marshall Plan for European recovery after the Second World War. After two years, he left to become President of the Ford Foundation. In 1953, Hoffman returned to Studebaker and oversaw its merger with the Packard Motor Company. In 1959 he became Executive Director of the newly created UN Special Fund. From January 1965, when the Special Fund was merged with EPTA, Hoffman became the first Administrator of UNDP, retiring in 1972 at the age of 81.

1972–75 Rudolph A. Peterson (United States)

Rudolph Peterson was born in Sweden and emigrated to the United States as a child. He spent his whole career in banking, in 1936 joining the Bank of America, where he remained for 20 years. He left to join the Bank of Honolulu, where he became President, returning to the Bank of America as Vice-Chairman in 1961 and then becoming its President and Chief Executive, retiring in 1969 when it was the biggest bank in America. On his retirement, President Richard Nixon asked him to chair a commission on international development which recommended more US support to multilateral aid. In 1972, he became the Administrator for a period of three years, while still acting as an adviser to the Bank of America in California.

1976–86 F. Bradford Morse (United States)

"Brad" Morse studied at Boston University, went into law practice after his LL.B., and returned to teach at Boston in 1949 as a Professor of Law. In 1952, he was elected to Lowell City Council (Massachusetts), and the following year he moved to Washington, where he was engaged in various capacities as an assistant on Capitol Hill, including staff member of the Senate Armed Services Committee and deputy administrator of the Veterans' Administration. In 1961, he was elected as a Republican Congressman to the US House of Representatives, where he served successive terms until 1972. In that year, he was appointed as UN under-Secretary-General for Political and General Assembly Affairs, a post he held for four years before becoming UNDP's longest-serving Administrator in 1976. After leaving the UN 10 years later, Morse became president of the Salzburg Global Seminar, a non-profit organization based in Austria.

1986–93 William H. Draper (United States)

Bill Draper spent most of his professional life in venture capital. After graduating from Yale University, he served as a second lieutenant in the Korean War, afterwards attending Harvard Business School. His first job was at the Inland Steel Company in Chicago, where he worked from 1954 to 1959 as a salesman. He then left to join his father's venture capital company, Draper, Gaither and Anderson, co-founding his own company, Draper and Johnson, after three years. In 1965, Draper set up Sutter Hill ventures and remained there as its senior partner for many years, supporting several hundred high-technology companies. In 1981, he was appointed by President Ronald Reagan to the US Export–Import Bank, where he served as President and Chairman until 1986, when he was appointed as Administrator. After leaving UNDP in 1993, Draper continued his venture capital activities, founding several new investment companies.

1993–99 James Gustave Speth (United States)

"Gus" Speth graduated from Yale Law School in 1969, having spent a year at Oxford University as a Rhodes scholar. He served as law clerk to the US Supreme Court, and in 1970 he was co-founder of the Natural Resources Defense Council, where he was senior attorney. From 1977 to 1981, Speth was a member and then Chairman of President Jimmy Carter's Council on Environmental Quality, and acted as the President's principal adviser on environmental matters. In 1981 he became Professor of Law at Georgetown University, and in 1982 he founded the World Resources Institute in Washington, DC and served as its president until 1993. In 1991, he was part of President-elect Bill Clinton's transition team, heading a group that examined US policy in natural resources and the environment. In 1993, he left the World Resources Institute to become Administrator. After leaving UNDP in 1999, he returned to Yale University as Dean of the School of Forestry.

1999–2005 Mark Malloch Brown (United Kingdom)

After studying at the Universities of Cambridge and Michigan, Mark Malloch Brown joined *The Economist* as a political correspondent, founding *The Economist Development Report*. He then joined the UN High Commission for Refugees, with which he worked in Thailand. In 1986, he joined the Sawyer-Miller Group in New York as a political and communications consultant, assisting candidates in presidential campaigns in Chile, the Philippines, and elsewhere. In 1994 he joined the World Bank, where he became Vice-President for External Affairs, a post that also carried responsibility for relations with the UN. In 1999 he was appointed Administrator, and from 2005 he held this post concurrently with the position of *Chef de Cabinet* of Secretary-General Kofi Annan. He left UNDP later that year when his successor was appointed, and became UN Deputy Secretary-General the following year, leaving the UN at the end of 2006.

2005–09 Kemal Dervis (Turkey)

Fluent in four languages (English, French, and German, in addition to Turkish), Kemal Dervis studied economics at the London School of Economics and earned a PhD from Princeton University. From 1973 to 1977 he taught at the Middle East Technical University and then at Princeton University. In 1977 he joined the World Bank, where he held various positions before becoming Vice-President for the Middle East and North Africa Region in 1996, and Vice-President for Poverty

Reduction and Economic Management in 2000. In 2001 he returned to Turkey where, as Minister for Economic Affairs, he was responsible for Turkey's recovery program after the financial crisis that hit the country in February 2001. Prior to his appointment with UNDP, Mr Dervis was a member of the Turkish Parliament from November 2002 to June 2005. He published extensively throughout his career on development subjects and globalization, and resigned in 2009 to return to research.

2009– Helen Clark (New Zealand)

After graduating from the University of Auckland, Helen Clark went on to teach political studies there. In 1981 she was elected to parliament, and in 1987 she was appointed to her first post as minister, first for conservation and housing, then for health and labor. She became Deputy Prime Minister in 1989, and went into opposition in 1993, becoming Deputy Leader of the Opposition and then Leader of the Opposition until winning the national election in November 1999. She then served three successive terms as New Zealand's Prime Minister until 2008, with concurrent responsibility for arts, culture, and heritage. During her terms, the country achieved significant economic growth, low unemployment, and high levels of investment in health and education. She was also a vocal campaigner for the rights of indigenous peoples, and for environmental sustainability. As Prime Minister, Helen Clark was a member of the Council of Women World Leaders, an international network of current and former women presidents and prime ministers, pressing for collective action on issues of critical importance to women and equitable development.

UNDP; Craig N. Murphy, *The United Nations Development Programme: A Better Way?* (Cambridge: Cambridge University Press, 2006); www.wikipedia.org

been taken up—as well as imitated by other development organizations—in a growing number of countries. Although its overall impact has been modest, it tapped into a rich source of know-how, with many countries demonstrating the value of the expertise and connection of their diaspora.

During this period, UNDP also adopted a practice, pioneered by UNICEF country offices, of recruiting national officers. To some traditionalists in the organization, for whom the UN's main role in TA was to provide expertise and services specifically unavailable in a country, it seemed like the wrong form of patronage, which contributed to an additional kind of (in situ) brain drain. However, the very rapid expansion in the numbers of local staff—who now form the overwhelming majority of the professionals working as staff (and not just consultants and experts) in UNDP—had at least two positive consequences. In the first place, it provided UNDP and other UN partners with qualified expertise at much less expense, while helping to bridge local linguistic and cultural divides. Secondly, national officers received training and were exposed to UN practices, helping them to develop professional skills that they could put to good use if they were either reabsorbed into local labor markets or "internationalized" through UNDP assignments abroad. In the latter case, they carried their home experience to other countries and helped to strengthen the role of UNDP's network of offices as a mechanism of exchange.

Conclusion

The failure of the Capacity Study to remodel the UN development system was a missed opportunity. Had the reform succeeded, UNDP would have played a central role and could have helped to shore up the system's effectiveness. It would be several more years before it began again to burnish its credentials as putative head of an increasingly dispersed UN family.

UNDP nevertheless enjoyed a highly innovative and productive first 15 years, albeit as an increasingly autonomous organization. Strong support from donors facilitated its expansion into many new areas. UNDP had become the quintessential doer, rather than thinker, remaining aloof from the ideological debates around the NIEO in which other parts of the system—notably UNCTAD—had become embroiled. It was not until later that UNDP began to worry about "standing for something."[69]

2　The 1980s and 1990s

- The Washington Consensus
- Breaking with the past
- Cost-sharing
- Other innovations
- Unified UN Offices, 1992–94
- Human development
- When human development caught on
- A policy organization?
- A greener organization
- The UN Development Group
- Conclusion

The 1970s had been the era of North–South confrontation. But in the following decade, the UN was in retreat before an unfavorable development climate and the ascendance of economic conservatism on a global scale. A new head of UNDP seemed steeped in the same mold, until he facilitated the emergence of a new paradigm that helped to turn the development debate back towards the UN.

This chapter recounts how "human development" was born under an unlikely midwife, how it influenced the organization to pay more attention to policy, and how UNDP subsequently developed expertise in environment and energy. It was also a period during which UNDP first turned inwards to address its own modernization, distancing itself further from the rest of the UN development system. Under a new Administrator, who was appointed as *de facto* development deputy to the UN Secretary-General, it then came back toward the center.

The Washington Consensus

The 1980s are sometimes known as the "lost decade" of development, at least for two of the world's major regions: Latin America and

Africa. The huge global savings surpluses that accumulated during the previous decade, in large part as a result of the unspent earnings of the oil-exporting countries, were recycled through private bank lending to developing countries, particularly in Latin America. When "stagflation" hit the developed countries in the early 1980s, interest rates went up. With the higher costs of borrowing and declining overseas markets, some Latin American countries were saddled with unaffordable debt burdens. In 1982, Mexico defaulted on its debt payments, and the region entered a period of retrenchment. The large economies of the region suffered negative per capita growth and a widespread fall in living standards. African countries were also hit hard by higher oil prices and a fall in the prices of their key export commodities as a result of global recession in the early part of the decade. In sub-Saharan Africa, per capita income declined by over 1 percent annually, food production fell by 20 percent overall, and human indicators of health and education enrollment also deteriorated.

The liquidity crisis forced the poor and vulnerable developing countries into the arms of the international financial institutions, the International Monetary Fund (IMF) and the World Bank in particular. Because bail-outs from the IMF were short-term, rapid retrenchment was prescribed in order to close the domestic and external funding gaps. This meant harsh cuts in public-sector spending, and economic and financial liberalization. On its heels, the World Bank sought to put in place structural reforms designed to sustain the solvency of the lenders. It conditioned its longer-term lending on "structural adjustment loans," beginning with Colombia in 1980, but soon extending to many other borrowing countries.

The IMF/World Bank prescriptions became known retrospectively as the "Washington Consensus."[1] And because of the strict conditionalities built into concessional lending extended to the poorer countries, the Bretton Woods institutions dominated the development agenda during the decade. They had the support of the US and UK governments and some other western donors—also major shareholders—who began to incorporate similar conditions into their own development programs.

Fiscal balancing led to cuts in health and education budgets, and the trade-off meant that economic and social development were now in different camps. The economic camp in Washington saw the crisis from a different vantage point from the social camp represented by UNDP, UNICEF and other field-based agencies, which witnessed deteriorating human conditions at first hand. Initially, the UN development system played only a bit-part in the policy debate which the bankers had monopolized. Then, in mid-decade, a group of development specialists convened by UNICEF began to examine more closely the human impact of the crisis in ten developing countries. The result was a path-breaking work called *Adjustment with a Human Face*, a poignant *cri de coeur* that helped to highlight the human costs of structural adjustment.[2] The chapter headings themselves are illustrative of the concerns raised by the book: "Economic Decline and Human Welfare in the First Half of the 1980s"; "Adjustment Policies 1980–85: Effects on Child Welfare"; "Adjustment at the Household Level: Potentials and Limitations of Survival Strategies." Perhaps more than any other book to that date, it marked the contrast in development paradigms between the World Bank and the UN—two parts of an extended family, but further apart in their respective approaches than at any other time.

Africa became the main battle-ground for adjustment versus social development. In 1981, the World Bank had published a report entitled *Accelerated Development in Sub-Saharan Africa*,[3] which "put most of the blame for Africa's economic crisis on African governments' support of public ownership and regulated markets" and downplayed the importance of external shocks from rising debt and declining trade.[4] At about the same time, the Organization for African Unity (OAU) and the UN Economic Commission for Africa (ECA) began working on a "Lagos Plan of Action" for African recovery. With this Plan and the publication of UNICEF's report, the UN had staked out a markedly different approach to the continent's problems, putting much greater emphasis on easing global financial and trading conditions and improving human conditions.

UNDP also deepened its involvement in Africa during the decade. It helped to finance the OAU/ECA work, and provided support to individual African governments in finding appropriate policy responses to their problems. As tradition dictated, however, UNDP did not take sides in the debate on structural adjustment, but then appeared to compromise its neutrality when, in 1988, it became the principal initial funder (with the African Development Bank and bilateral donors) of a World Bank-executed program called Social Dimensions of Adjustment (SDA). For some within the UN system, including in UNDP itself, SDA appeared to be providing a light blue cloak of respectability to a controversial World Bank approach, especially because UNDP's influence over the program was limited. For its sister agencies, UNDP appeared to be breaking ranks. But in terms of family harmony, much worse was to come.

Breaking with the past

In 1984, Morse himself became more involved in Africa, when the Secretary-General asked him to head concurrently the new UN Office for Emergency Operations in Africa (OEOA), created to provide a response to the humanitarian crisis in many countries, again largely as a result of drought. In 1986 he left UNDP, to be replaced by another American, nominated by a Republican administration.

William H. Draper III had spent most of his professional life as a venture capitalist, then serving as president of the US Export–Import Bank for five years before joining UNDP. Like Peterson, he may have seemed a curious choice for a UN development position. As Reagan's nominee, he was of a distinctly conservative persuasion, and a strong believer in free markets and the private sector. He thus entered the scene seemingly on the "wrong" side of the development debate, just as it was becoming increasingly ideological. Few foresaw then that he would go on to become one of the most visionary of UNDP's Administrators.

Draper spent his first months discovering UNDP and the system. But quite early on, he began to urge on his colleagues the virtues of working with the private sector. Word went out to all the country offices to try to engage with a new set of partners and make it clear that UNDP was supportive of private enterprise. This strident attachment to the importance of the private sector—especially at a time when controversial programs of liberalization were only just beginning in the United States and Europe—caused initial discomfort and some resistance among many of Draper's colleagues. There was little knowledge, and some mistrust, of private enterprise, and for the purists, the notion of using public money to support the profit-motivated was anathema.

In fact, Draper's intentions were more pragmatic than ideological. He was ahead of his time in UNDP, with its almost exclusive focus on public institutions, when other parts of the UN system already had programs with the private sector. The International Trade Centre (ITC) in Geneva counted small enterprises as its principal beneficiaries,[5] and the ILO[6] and the UN Industrial Development Organization had active entrepreneur training programs.

In retrospect, Draper was correct in identifying private enterprise as the main agent of development change. For several decades, governments had been given the benefit of the doubt as managers of the development process. But growing skepticism about the effectiveness of aid[7] in non-performing developing countries cast growing doubt on the wisdom of entrusting development management to counterparts in the public sector. Governments of some of the poorest countries were not viewed as paragons of progress, with their patrimonial traditions, lack of accountability, and inherent mistrust of private initiative. By concentrating almost exclusively on the public sector, development organizations failed to recognize that the real targets of their assistance—the vast majority of the poor—were struggling for survival in their own private commercial environments, in which governments were more of a hindrance than a help.

Draper's advocacy of private enterprise had rather limited impact in UNDP, at least during his own tenure. The main outcome was a change in image, an organization that was no longer set apart from the practical world of business. One consequence was an increase in the numbers of applicants for UN jobs from people in the private sector, or who would have been expecting to apply for private-sector jobs.

Draper grew quickly into the UNDP job, but he had little time or patience with the rest of the UN system. He wanted to rebrand UNDP under the rubric "World Development," and dropped the UN emblem from the letterhead because he deliberately promoted the organization as a more independent entity. There were at least two motivations for this. The first was image: the UN at that time was not held in high esteem by the US administration, and some of the agencies were poorly managed by long-entrenched incumbents and had lost the confidence of some major donors.[8] The second was more of a business matter. Draper was unwilling to channel funds through agencies to execute projects if he thought he could get better value outside the system.

From the late 1980s onwards, UNDP began deliberately to withdraw funding from the agencies. For the larger agencies, such as WHO, FAO, and ILO, which had already established other sources of support for their TA activities, withdrawal was relatively painless. But some smaller UN organizations—such as UNCTAD, ITC, and the five regional commissions—initially found it difficult to accommodate to the loss of revenue. Draper also encouraged UNFPA to become more independent, with its own financial and administrative arrangements, and the appointment of its own country directors (instead of representation by UNDP at the field level). UNDP also began to build up expertise in different specialized fields, including several covered by other UN agencies (such as agriculture, health, and environment), and the organization began to resemble a microcosm of the rest of the system. During this period, the different parts of the UN development system were further apart than ever. Globally, UNDP had become more isolated and mistrusted than at any other time, even as coordinating mechanisms were being established to try to bring the system into better alignment at country level. It was a risky strategy because, in trying to be a more complete development organization, UNDP opened itself to direct competition with the World Bank, an intellectually and financially more powerful rival.

Cost-sharing

In its own way, however, UNDP had become a more effective development organization. The funding situation remained relatively healthy. Annual voluntary pledges peaked at US$1.2 billion in 1989,[9] a record level that has never been achieved since, even in nominal terms. But income was now being supplemented by new sources, and in particular from developing country "cost-sharing."

In the 1980s, the Latin American countries began to forge a rather different relationship with UNDP. During that difficult decade, the countries of the region were being held back by inefficient public administrations, just when effective management was critically needed. In 1983, the UNDP representative in Argentina saw an opportunity to convince the main political protagonists of the need for major reforms of the public sector. Using the principle of national execution (NEX), already in extensive use, he convinced the government to channel funds (from World Bank and Inter-American Bank loans as well as from its own sources) through UNDP for the purposes of hiring professional staff and procuring equipment.[10] Through UNDP, staff could be offered more competitive salaries and equipment could be purchased in a more timely and cost-effective manner. The public administration was an obvious beneficiary, at least in the short term. Argentina's development partners also supported any measures to strengthen public services, and the development banks could anticipate a faster and more efficient disbursement of their loans.

This practice of "100 percent cost-sharing" was taken up by other countries of the region, including Brazil, Peru, and Paraguay; by some Central American countries (Honduras, Panama, Guatemala, and El Salvador); and by Bulgaria and Egypt in other regions. This (non-core) source is, in most years, larger than UNDP's core income (from regular donors). Having countries purchase services from UNDP in this manner is a much better guarantee that TA needs will be satisfied than purchasing through the traditional pre-funded aid modality. It also helps maintain high standards in UNDP as the supplier of services. What is of greater concern, however, is that countries will utilize UNDP as an ongoing alternative administration and procurement system, which is parallel to their own and which does not contribute to domestic capacity development.

In the same decade, questions of capacity began to preoccupy UNDP. This was not "capacity" in the Jackson sense, which had more to do with empowering the UN system to manage its resources well. It was about creating capacity for development in the countries themselves. Within the Africa Bureau, a group began work on a program, euphemistically called National Technical Cooperation Assessments and Programming, the objective of which was to examine the real impact of TA in leaving behind enhanced capacity of individuals and institutions. The national studies conducted were not very sanguine about the results of TA, and in 1993, UNDP produced a book which was rather self-critical.[11] It appeared to embarrass a lot of people in UNDP, but contributed to a rethinking of the traditional forms of TA, until then mainly characterized by missions of foreign experts and formal training events.

Less than ten years later, some of the same individuals in UNDP returned to the subject, launching a major program of research, which included several national and international consultations, culminating in the publication of three books.[12] This work on capacity development was significant because it began to vest UNDP—essentially a spending and doing organization—with more depth and a greater sense of purpose. Capacity development was taken up subsequently as UNDP's principal operational *raison d'être*.

Other innovations

Draper also recognized that differentiating UNDP from the rest of the system meant modernizing and professionalizing the staff. He devoted more of the organization's resources to training, and brought in specialists to deliver in-house courses in management techniques to middle-ranking and higher grades. Not content with passive methods of recruitment, he asked staff to visit the campuses of top western universities and encourage their students to apply. One result was to greatly increase the number of applicants to the new "young professionals" program which UNDP started.

In order to strengthen corporate coherence, Draper established an Action Committee which he chaired every week to review and approve larger projects emanating from HQ and the field. The committee was attended by all the senior managers of the organizations, but presentations were made by the project staff. There were several benefits. Approval criteria could be applied more uniformly across the organization. Different regions could become familiar with each other's work. Staff had to prepare convincing and concise justifications for their projects (often on behalf of colleagues in country offices). And it allowed Draper and the managers to become more familiar with the rank and file.

One of the approval criteria which was receiving growing emphasis was an attention to the concerns of women, which Draper championed. In 1978, a UN Fund for Women (UNIFEM) had been established under the management authority of UNDP. UNIFEM tended in practice to work in parallel to UNDP, even setting up its own network of field representatives, and Draper saw fit to establish a Women in Development Division within the organization. One of its roles was to ensure that projects were sufficiently sensitive to women's needs. With the advent of the human development paradigm, gender concerns gained even greater importance.[13]

Draper also sought to promote greater gender equality through the appointment of competent women. He brought in Ellen Sirleaf-Johnson to head the African Bureau, a former banker and Liberian finance minister, and one of the first women to become Assistant Secretary-General in UNDP. After leaving UNDP, she was elected President of Liberia in 2005, the first-ever female African head of state. Draper was not surprised.[14] As head of the Women's Division, he appointed Ingrid Eide, a noted Norwegian scholar. In the field, he also sought to raise the then low proportion of women resident representatives (they now make up a third of the total).

Unified UN Offices, 1992–94

The implosion of the Soviet Union at the end of 1991 brought a new set of independent countries into the UN. For the development system, they were the so-called "transition economies" of the Commonwealth of Independent States. UNDP and the UN agencies had very limited experience or understanding of these countries, but the most immediate preoccupation was a humanitarian one, as comprehensive economic collapse was swiftly followed by a breakdown in health, education, housing and other public support services. The region saw the most rapid peacetime fall in human development indicators in modern history.

In 1992, Draper took a decision that appeared at the time to belie sober judgment, but which also turned out to be far-sighted. He resolved to establish offices in all of the 11 newly independent republics and the three Baltic states (and later in the Russian Federation itself). Preparatory missions were sent out, and during 1992 the first offices were being opened (in Belarus, Latvia, and Ukraine). Draper persuaded the Secretary-General of the wisdom of UN representation in these new states, which were desirous to demonstrate the value they attached to membership of the world organization. There were no funds earmarked for these offices, and the governing council was quite reluctant about the decision. But the new missions were nonetheless established as joint ventures between UNDP and the UN's Department of Public Information. The heads of each office were designated as UN Representatives and, for the first time since the 1960s, there was unified UN representation at the country level.

Given the heightened rivalry among agencies, which Draper had done little to discourage, the unified concept was endangered from the outset. The Secretary-General was unable to persuade the General Assembly to confirm the unified status of these offices, which he had proposed to be headed by UN Ambassadors. Within two years, after aggressive lobbying of permanent representatives in New York by other UN organizations and agencies, additional UN representative offices were permitted to open in the same countries. The last best hope for genuinely unified UN field representation—which has been repeatedly urged as the centerpiece of UN development system reform—had disappeared.

Human development

Draper will be remembered by many people in the UN, not primarily as the champion of the private sector and the modernizer of UNDP, but as the person who insisted on giving the organization something to stand for, thus helping to complete its transformation into a more comprehensive development agency. His espousal of advocacy led him to back the Human Development Reports. The decision to promote a radical social agenda could not have been presaged from Draper's conservative background. Human development, however, turned out to be a powerful development brand and became the best descriptor of an organization which had always had difficulty defining itself.

The first Human Development Report (HDR) appeared in 1990. Because of its timing, the appearance of the report might have seemed like another UN riposte to Washington orthodoxy. But to that point, UNDP had no known track record as a pioneer of development thinking (some insiders claiming that it had always been "anti-intellectual" in its operational approach). Even though it satisfied Draper's quest for UNDP to find something to "believe in,"[15] the human development initiative had accidental origins.

The report was the brainchild of a Pakistani and ex-World Bank economist, Mahbub ul Haq, who had met Draper in New York and impressed him with his vision of a new development paradigm. Although human development as a concept would not have been within the compass of his pro-business mind, Draper nevertheless gave ul Haq a position in UNDP as his Special Advisor, and the resources and staff he needed to write a report on the "human condition." The first HDR that resulted had a huge impact. In part, it was the message it conveyed and the manner in which it was presented. The concept itself was not new, and had been anticipated by ul Haq, Amartya Sen, and others some years before.[16] But there were several special factors that made the report an immediate success. One was that the world was ready for its ideas. There had been growing disillusion with the predominance of economic growth as a yardstick of development progress and a concern—eloquently raised by UNICEF in its 1987 book on *Adjustment with a Human Face*—for human welfare as the principal development goal.[17] Economic growth enlarged the size of the economy, but did not guarantee greater well-being, particularly for the marginalized populations. The second factor was the inclusion in the report of a "human development index," which for the first time ranked countries in terms of a proxy for well-being rather than the clinical and ambiguous measure of income per head. A third factor had to do with presentation. The reports were lucidly written and highly relevant to contemporary challenges, and UNDP organized a very well-publicized global launch of the report, along with an embargo date, press kits, and conferences. This helped to generate media coverage on a scale unprecedented for any UN product.

The central concept was simple but powerful (see Box 2.1). People were not the means to development ends, they were themselves the ends. For years, development apostles of the left had been putting people at the centre, but ul Haq's report captured more fully the idea of a people-centered approach by the simple but more fundamental notion of widening people's choices and strengthening their capabilities. If people—from the poorest all the way up the social scale—had more choices and could exercise more control over their own lives for the betterment of themselves and their families, then human development was advancing.

The Human Development Index (HDI) developed in the report was a reflection of human capabilities, comprising the three essential components of longevity, knowledge, and decent living standards. Each of these capabilities was measured by a proxy: longevity by life expectancy at birth, knowledge by literacy rates,[18] and living standards by

Box 2.1 Human development defined

Human development is a process of enlarging people's choices. In principle, these choices can be infinite and change over time. But at all levels of development, the three essential choices are for people to lead a long and healthy life; to acquire knowledge; and to have access to resources needed for a decent standard of living. If these essential choices are not available, many other opportunities remain inaccessible. But human development does not end there. Additional choices, highly valued by many people, range from political, economic, and social freedom to opportunities for being creative and productive, and enjoying personal self-respect and guaranteed human rights.

Human development has two sides: the formation of human capabilities—such as improved health, knowledge, and skills; and the use people make of their acquired capabilities—for leisure, productive purposes, or being active in cultural, social, and political affairs. If the scales of human development do not finely balance the two sides, considerable human frustration may result. According to this concept of human development, income is clearly only one option that people would like to have, albeit an important one. But it is not the sum total of their lives. Development must therefore be more than just the expansion of income and wealth. Its focus must be people.

UNDP, *Human Development Report 1990* (Oxford: Oxford University Press, 1990)

per capita income. The HDI placed countries on a scale determined by minimum and maximum values for each variable and then averaged the three. As the report admitted, these proxies were more convenient than comprehensive, and were chosen partly because of widely available statistics. In future years, the HDI methodology was refined (although this did not prevent a lingering controversy over the interpretation of the index, and issues such as the weighting of its components).

But the publication of the HDI had immediate and controversial results. Countries were ranked not by a single, sterile economic metric, but by human-performance indicators. Thus some low-income countries, such as China and Sri Lanka, had relatively high HDIs, while some high-income countries, such as some of the Gulf States, had low HDIs. Some developing countries objected strongly to the implications of the report and its HDI. Malaysia walked out of the UNDP

Governing Council, and Oman later withdrew entirely from UNDP over the findings of HDRs (and did not return).

Draper himself had misgivings about the first HDR, although—in true Voltairian style—he steadfastly supported the independence of ul Haq's work. He was disappointed that the United States had not come highest in the HDI ranking (it was 19th out of 130, one above Israel) and, with a glance at the White House, much more disturbed by the elevated ranking of non-democracies such as Cuba (39th), China (65th), and Vietnam (75th). In the *Human Development Report 1991*, a Human Freedom Index was introduced, ranking countries according to their conformity with the 40 indicators of a "World Human Rights Guide." On this index, the non-democracies all fared badly. But the index raised new controversies, the most serious being over human rights in such areas as homosexuality, and inter-racial and inter-religious marriage. Some developing countries claimed that the index reflected an exclusive set of western values.

The Human Freedom Index was dropped, but the HDRs and HDIs survived and thrived. For the first time, UNDP had a publication gaining headlines every year, and based on influential research which was cited as a development reference. The uptake of the concept within the organization, however, was slow. One reason was that—probably like most of the world[19]—staff had difficulty initially grasping the full meaning of the human development concept. There was a tendency to equate it with human *resource* development—in other words, the productivity aspect, as opposed to the comprehensive human focus. The other reason was that the HDR Office was placed, physically and organizationally, outside UNDP, since it was politically more acceptable to designate the HDRs as reports to, rather than of, the organization. Partly as a result, and despite decisions by the governing council to make human development the central programming ideal of UNDP, the HDR Office and its staff were not considered as integral parts of UNDP, and the ideas were not mainstreamed into programs for several years, and even then only partially.

In terms of the narrative of this book, the human development initiative did little to bridge UNDP's isolation within the system. In spite of its timeliness and originality, it was considered to be a specific UNDP brand, but not a UN one, even if some of the thinking was influential. Agency pride and the increasingly autonomous status of UNDP were partly to blame. But it was symptomatic of one of the UN development system's most serious failings: an inability to find a common language and a common agenda—with the possible later exception of the Millennium Declaration of 2000 and its Millennium

Development Goals (MDGs).[20] If anything, UNDP's most significant influence may have been on the World Bank, which began to incorporate the language of human development into its own operations and organizational designations. Unfortunately, however, there was little evidence that the World Bank really took the concept on board—"human" development seemed merely to be a redesignation of "social" development. There was no such ambiguity in the IMF, which appeared to ignore the language and the concept entirely.[21]

In 1995, the Secretary-General produced *An Agenda for Development*[22] in an attempt to give more focus to the work of the UN development system. And in the same year, the UN staged two major conferences. The first was the World Summit on Social Development in Copenhagen, where "governments reached a new consensus on the need to put people at the centre of development." In fact the consensus was not very "new" and "social development" was still the language of the 1945 UN Charter. Rather surprisingly, there is no mention at all of human development in any of the 132 pages of the conference report and declaration.[23] The second global event was the Beijing Conference on Women, where the HDR was more influential. UNDP had wisely devoted its HDR in that year to women's issues, refining its Gender Development Index. While the conference declaration made no more than a passing mention of human development (just two references), the findings of the report helped to highlight the many challenges facing women. The graphic cover illustrated that women's total economic contributions were greater than men's.

When human development caught on

After the first HDR appeared in 1990, there were doubts both inside and outside the organization about whether there was enough original research to support an annual publication, which inevitably was compared (rather favorably) to the World Development Report, which the World Bank had been producing annually since 1978.

These doubts were soon allayed: one of the HDR's successes has been its continuity and the use of the concept to interpret the human development aspects of key development concerns, many neglected by the World Bank, and some of which the UN had hitherto been reluctant to tackle. The second report in 1991 looked at the financial requirements to meet human development goals; the 1992 report examined the human development implications of the inequitable global economy; in 1993, it was people's participation, and so on (Table 2.1). For the first few years, there were also refinements in the

Table 2.1 Human Development Reports: main topics

	Topics	New indices
1990	Concept and measurement of HD	Human Development Index (HDI)
1991	Financing HD	Human Freedom Index (HFI), Gender-sensitive HDI (GDI), Distribution-adjusted HDI
1992	Global dimensions of HD	
1993	People's participation	HDI for different population groups within countries
1994	Human security	HDI for different sub-national regions
1995	Gender	Gender Empowerment Measure (GEM)
1996	Economic growth and HD	
1997	Poverty eradication	Human Poverty Index (HPI)
1998	Consumption for HD	
1999	Globalization with a human face	
2000	Human rights and HD	
2001	New technologies and HD	
2002	Democracy in a fragmented world	
2003	Millennium Development Goals	
2004	Cultural liberty	
2005	Aid, trade, and security	
2006	Global water crisis	
2007/8	Climate change	
2009	Migration	
2010	Twenty years of human development	Inequality-adjusted HDI, Gender Inequality Index (GII) Multi-dimensional Poverty Index (MPI)

HDI and the addition of other indices. The ranking of country performance was to become a permanent feature, and the HDRs made good use of statistics in order to dramatize its messages. The HDR was also successful in enlisting some eminent contemporary thinkers and political leaders to contribute to the analysis. Amartya Sen, Hans Singer, Richard Jolly, Frances Stewart, Gustav Ranis, and others collaborated closely with Mahbub ul Haq, and continued to contribute to the report after his departure in 1995.[24] Every report since 1994 has also included contributions by senior figures. In that year, the report was on human security and included short essays by five Nobel laureates. In 1995, there were contributions from seven serving female heads of state or government.

Notwithstanding their relative isolation within the system, the HDRs made original and well-timed inputs to global development debates. The 1997 report helped to define poverty in a much more comprehensive manner, emphasizing the many forms of deprivation besides lack of income. In 1999, the HDR addressed the phenomenon of globalization, appearing just months before street demonstrations by detractors brought the WTO ministerial conference in Seattle, United States to a halt. The following year, the report looked in depth at human rights issues, which were shown to be inseparable from development goals. In 2002, the HDR tackled democracy, and in 2004, culture; in more recent years, it has focused on the environment. Over time, the boundaries of the human development paradigm have widened, but more importantly, the human development approach has been applied to national problems in countries in all parts of the world.

From 1992, starting with Bangladesh, Colombia, and Pakistan, UNDP country offices began to generate "national HDRs" as local initiatives. Because there was no tradition of research in UNDP, and no centralized mechanism of quality control, the standard of analysis in these reports was at first very uneven, and the themes only loosely connected to the human development concept. It was several years before the majority of these reports could pass muster—and only from the reports of 1999 do the contents of these national HDRs appear on UNDP's website.[25] An important benefit, however, was the engagement of country offices with local research bodies, enhancing UNDP's profile as an interlocutor of policy-makers. One of the countries that most warmly embraced the human development approach was India. Only one national HDR was produced there (in 2002), but from the mid-1990s they were produced for a growing number of individual Indian states. The state of Madhya Pradesh alone, under a dynamic Chief Minister, produced three reports between 1995 and 2002, featuring the calculation of district-level HDIs, which acted as barometers for the local impact of public policies. In Brazil, HDIs were calculated at municipal level, generating widespread awareness of HDI and much political questioning when some areas were shown to be doing better than others.

Then, in 2000, a new team began to develop what many have considered the most influential piece of analysis ever to come out of UNDP. Mark Malloch Brown, the Administrator since 1999, had appointed Rima Khalaf Hunaidi, a former planning minister of

Jordan, as the head of the Arab States Bureau. She worked with a research group led by an eminent Egyptian political scientist, Nader Fergany,[26] and, with the support of the Arab Fund for Economic and Social Development, produced the first Arab HDR in 2002. The report examined the state of human development in the 22 Arab States and, true to the standards of the global reports, its findings were unvarnished and well corroborated with available data. This report "by Arabs for Arabs" (as UNDP described it) duly recorded the progress that the region had made in terms of some of the human development indicators. But it poignantly described the problems of the region:

> The predominant characteristic of the current Arab reality seems to be the existence of deeply rooted shortcomings in Arab institutional structures. These shortcomings pose serious obstacles to human development and are summarized as the three deficits relating to freedom, empowerment of women, and knowledge. They constitute weighty constraints on human capability that must be lifted.[27]

This report also had an immediate impact. It was downloaded from the UNDP website (in Arabic and English) more than a million times, and widely read and discussed. The Arab press praised it. The *Middle East Quarterly* wrote that "with uncommon candor and a battery of statistics, the report tells a sorry story of two decades of failed planning and developmental decline. One inescapable conclusion emerges from its sober pages of tables and charts: the Arab world is in decline, even relative to the developing world."[28] The Egyptian *Al-Ahram Weekly* recommended the report because "no changes will occur without Arabs first facing the facts, however unpalatable they may be."[29] The western press, attempting to interpret the Arab world only months after 9/11, was equally positive. *Time* magazine called it "perhaps the most important volume published in 2002";[30] and *The New York Times*: "if you want to understand the milieu that produced bin Ladenism, and will reproduce it if nothing changes, read this report."[31]

The Arab HDR became an annual publication for its first four years. Having identified the "deficits" of freedom, women's empowerment, and knowledge, the next three editions went into each of them in more depth. The 2004 report (on "freedom") tipped over into even greater controversy when (like the third global HDR in 1992) it also looked at the international dimensions of human development in the region. It was openly critical of the occupation of Palestine and Iraq, and courted the wrath of the US State Department. After a long delay, the report went out, but the Administrator felt constrained to state that "some of the views expressed by the authors are not shared by UNDP or the UN."

A policy organization?

With the HDRs, UNDP had elaborated a path-breaking concept and discovered the power of advocacy, leading UNDP inexorably into the policy arena, where before it had been uncertain to tread. The ILO had nearly 200 labor standards and conventions. The UN secretariat had drawn up the Convention on the Elimination of All Forms of Discrimination Against Women in 1979. UNICEF had developed the almost universally adopted Convention on the Rights of the Child in 1989.[32] Many other UN bodies had developed standards and norms. UNDP now had human development goals—encapsulated by the HDI—which were far more ambitious.

The paradigm was too imprecise to provide benchmarks of compliance. But UNDP could have persevered to develop such benchmarks country by country, and anticipated by several years a version of the MDGs (which were formalized in 2000). But UNDP was still fundamentally an organization of project management and, while it succeeded in enunciating human development approaches at the regional level, there was no central organizational drive—nor the inclination in its country offices—to benchmark country performance. During the 1990s, even the mainstreaming of the concept into its project work was not achieved. In spite of the proliferation of national HDRs and guidelines on the "operationalization" of human development, the culture of UNDP—highly dispersed among the staff of over 100 offices worldwide—was not amenable to such change. Instead, a kind of professional caste system was developing with UNDP bifurcated into HQ-based thinkers and field-based doers. The ideas—like the staff—rarely crossed the divide.

In HQ, a second research unit was established by the departing first director of the HDR Office. In a new manifestation of intellectual *laissez faire*, the Office of Development Studies was given a budget to commence research in 1997 on international cooperation, bringing together some eminent minds around the subject of global public goods. In 1999, the work resulted in a highly praised book on the subject, comprising chapters by Amartya Sen, Joseph Stiglitz, Jeffrey Sachs, and others.[33] It was a field of research wholly different from human development, but the book blazed an important trail in anticipating what became the fastest-growing new area of development cooperation. It was followed by a second book a few years later, written by some of the same authors.[34] The office also sponsored a high-quality book on the Tobin Tax, with equally eminent authors, including the Nobel laureate economist James Tobin himself. Unfortunately, owing to US legislation to the effect that all American funding should be withdrawn immediately from any UN agency promoting ideas or policies that might have a financial impact unfavorable to citizens or other bodies of the United States, this publication had to be published privately and launched in the United Kingdom.

UNDP now had two offices doing high-quality research, both in an offshore mode. Like the HDRs, the *Global Public Goods* book helped to ferment a constructive debate on a relatively immature subject, further burnishing UNDP's name in academic and policy circles. It was not pitched at UNDP's operations, however, and had little practical influence, even on the organization's global programs.

UNDP's Bureau for Development Policy was strengthened during Malloch Brown's tenure and was intended to be the organization's custodian of policy advice. In the past ten years, it has been organized around UNDP's main operational priorities, which have varied in number, but have included the core concerns of poverty reduction, democratic governance, environment and energy, and HIV/AIDS. (A fifth priority, crisis prevention and recovery, was given its own separate bureau.) Women's empowerment, human rights, and capacity development are designated as cross-cutting themes, so the policy teams in headquarters have embraced some of the main tenets of human development. It might have seemed logical to include the HDR Office and the Office of Development Studies[35] in the policy bureau, but both argued to maintain their independence, including the unit that oversaw the National and Regional HDRs. From the vantage point of headquarters, the *status quo* may have had its own justification. For the country offices, however—as the intended purveyors of UNDP policy advice—the rationale of separate offices was much less compelling.

In the new century, UNDP could now claim to be an organization of some substance. During Malloch Brown's tenure, the Bureau for Development Policy established a *Development Policy Journal* (which ran for three issues in 2002–03), and began preparing "policy notes" on a wide range of development topics—the original target was 200. The intention was to support UNDP's country offices in becoming more active as sources of policy advice. The policy notes duly began to appear, but their preparation was belabored by the difficulties of reaching a consensus on positions consistent with UN ideals and human development objectives. The question also arose as to whether UNDP's policy positions were identical to those of other UN entities.

A much more promising, and productive, initiative was the development of a series of global knowledge networks. Staff from any location were invited to subscribe electronically to one or more of the networks, which were established in each of UNDP's priority fields (or "practice areas"). The subscribers in each area (mostly numbering between 600 and 1,200) became known as communities of practice. The large majority of UNDP staff belonged to at least one of these communities. Through these networks, members received information about the subject area, but even more importantly, they could make requests for practical advice to which others in the same network responded, drawing on their own knowledge and experience. The manager of each network would then produce "consolidated responses," which would be posted for everyone to access.

The networks (Table 2.2) were the foundation of a knowledge management system unique within the UN system. They acted as a bridge between headquarters and the field, facilitated cross-country and cross-regional exchange, and enhanced the technical advisory capacities of

Table 2.2 Principal UNDP knowledge networks

Network name	Type of network	Membership type	Members (2005)
Crisis prevention and recovery	Development practice	UNDP	1,236
Democratic governance	Development practice	UNDP	1,348
Energy and environment	Development practice	UNDP	1,117
HIV/AIDS	Development practice	UNDP	806
Poverty reduction	Development practice	UNDP	1,244
Gender	Cross-cutting	UNDP	763
Millennium Development Goals	UN system	UNDP and other UN	2,340
Human Development Report	UN system	UNDP, UN, external	1,013
Human rights policy	UN system	UNDP	601

Source: UNDP Bureau for Development Policy internal document, 2005

country offices. By 2005, there were nine networks in substantive areas (and several additional sub-practice networks), as well as several more in areas of administrative and management interest.

The UNDP networks came in for a lot of praise.[36] They showed how a UN platform could be a powerful means of knowledge-sharing, building on practical experience. The networks also gave a stronger sense of global cohesion within UNDP. In order to reinforce the organization's new role, UNDP established regional service centers in strategic locations (see Chapter 4) and staffed them with policy advisers, but they were spread very thinly over the (by then) 130 country offices, and could not replace the ubiquity and convenience of the knowledge networks.

A generation earlier, Jackson's *Capacity Study* had devised an "information systems concept" which was never developed. UNDP's global networking was a modern electronic manifestation of it, albeit confined to one organization. Membership of the original networks was not opened up to other UN agencies. However, three newer electronic communities were created around the MDGs, HDRs, and human rights, inviting participants from other agencies. In 2010, UNDP adopted a new and more powerful electronic platform (called "teamworks") designed to boost the use of knowledge-sharing within the UN system.

A greener organization

Draper left UNDP in 1993 and was replaced by the founder and head of the World Resources Institute (WRI) in Washington, James Gustave Speth. Nominated by the Clinton White House (where he had a friend in Al Gore), Speth was neither Republican nor banker, but hailed from the ideological left. Unlike his predecessors, he came to the job with a background of development and some knowledge of UNDP, which had been a financial sponsor of WRI.

Gus Speth's arrival in UNDP was well-timed, as the 1990s saw an increase in concern for the global environment. In the first flush of environmental awareness, the UN had held an environment conference in Stockholm in 1972. The conference had led to the creation of the UN Environment Programme (UNEP) in the same year,[37] but global interest in the environment waned for the next decade.[38] Then, in 1985, arguably the most successful international agreement in the sphere of development was concluded in Vienna: the Vienna Convention for the Protection of the Ozone Layer. The convention was drawn up in response to a serious depletion of ozone in the Earth's atmosphere, which threatened human and animal health through increased ultra-violet radiation. The cause was the emission of chlorofluorocarbons (CFCs), and it led in 1987 to the Montreal Protocol, which set targets for steep cuts in CFCs.[39] The agreement and the protocol were successful in slowing down and reversing ozone depletion.

Also in 1987, the prestigious World Commission on Environment and Development, chaired by Gro Harlem Brundtland, Prime Minister of Norway, published its report: *Our Common Future*.[40] The report helped to embed the concerns of environmental sustainability firmly within the development agenda. One of the members of the Commission was the Canadian businessman and philanthropist Maurice Strong, who had been Secretary-General of the Stockholm conference and became the first Executive Director of UNEP.

The report, together with the success of the Montreal Protocol, were inducements to further action on the environment, and in 1992 the UN convened a second "Earth Summit" in Rio de Janeiro, with Maurice Strong again as Secretary-General. The meeting was a landmark event attended by 100 national leaders (heads of state or government). It resulted in three significant new agreements: the Convention on Biological Diversity, the Framework Agreement on Climate Change,[41] and *Agenda 21*, a blueprint for sustainable development. The Rio Summit also led to the formalization of the new Global Environment Facility as a tripartite fund managed by UNDP, the World Bank, and UNEP. The environment had thus become a lucrative new area of activity for the UN system, in which UNDP was now competing as an implementing agency. During the decade, UNDP built up a significant body of expertise in this area, and in terms of technical specializations the environment became UNDP's strongest suit, which it remains today. UNDP's bifurcation into both a funding and an implementing organization was more marked than ever.

Together with the multilateral fund established to support projects under the Montreal Protocol and funding for the *Agenda 21* program, UNDP was now able to tap into significant new sources of funding. These additional sources were all the more important because of a decline in core funding which dipped below $1US billion and never regained that level. During the 1990s, which had begun with a sharp fall in official development assistance,[42] the traditional donors began to more actively undermine the principles of multilateralism by providing more of their funding to development institutions on a conditional basis, usually targeting specific domains and sometimes tying procurement to the source. During the decade, the number of separate trust funds managed by UNDP grew to over 80.[43]

Gus Speth was responsible for "greening" UNDP, but there was another priority domain that he recognized as being of growing importance. A profiling of all the ongoing projects revealed that a high proportion of UNDP's activities were on public administration, electoral reform, decentralization, and other areas broadly within the area of governance. He therefore proposed that "good governance" be designated as one of the four major priority areas, along with poverty reduction, environmental management, and women in development. The term was sensitive for some of the program countries—and in official reports it was referred to by the rather cumbersome "enabling environment for sustainable human development"—but the Executive Board went along with the new focus. A fifth priority area, countries in special development situations, was added in recognition of the fact that UNDP was becoming more involved, in Burundi, Democratic Republic of Congo, Rwanda, and elsewhere, in post-conflict peace-building activities including repatriation and demobilization of combatants (see Table 3.1).

Organizationally, Speth's tenure was marked by a process of active reform. In 1996, he set in motion a comprehensive internal review, which came to be known as "UNDP 2001." One of the most notable innovations was the "results-oriented annual reports" (ROARs), which for the first time attempted to show clear links between the funding of projects and program outcomes. Precise attribution is always difficult in development cooperation. However, the ROARs were important in bringing a results-based approach to UNDP programming. Another consequence of the reform was a decentralization of core-funded posts from headquarters to the country offices, and the creation of several sub-regional resource facilities (SuRFs) designed to provide substantive support to programs in the field. The SuRFs were the forerunners of the much larger regional support centers that followed several years later.

The UN Development Group

Speth also demonstrated a stronger commitment to working with the rest of the UN development family, under the slogan "sustainable human development." The Secretary-General, Boutros Boutros-Ghali, designated him as *de facto* development chief and as chair of periodic meetings of the UN funds and programs development agencies. This was a significant move in re-establishing—at least in name—the *primus inter pares* role of UNDP, headed by (at the time) the system's most senior Under-Secretary-General.[44] It also meant that the long-standing tension between the UN Secretary-General and the UNDP Administrator over the supervision of the UN resident coordinators in the field was resolved in UNDP's favor. UNDP instituted the first resident coordinator assessment courses in 1998, to help prepare its own staff and those from other agencies for the resident coordinator role.

In 1997, as part of his own reform program, the incoming Secretary-General Kofi Annan built on this clustering arrangement and established four groups of UN agencies and organizations: so-called Executive Committees for Development, Economic and Social, Humanitarian, and Peace and Security matters. The main objectives of these ExComs was to ensure more frequent contact among UN entities. UNDP chaired the development ExCom (which became the UN Development Group, UNDG), and is represented on the three others. The distinctions between "development" and "economic and social" may seem ambiguous. In practice, however, development is taken to mean essentially field operations, while economic and social is concerned more with research and information. The UNDG, which has a secretariat (UN Development Operations Coordination Office) in the UNDP building, supports the UN resident coordinators and UN country teams in the field. Characteristically for the UN, membership of the UNDG has grown as much through accident as by design: there are no clear criteria for membership, which is the result of requests initiated by agencies and organizations. UNDG does not include every operational agency of the UN development system (for example, the quintessentially operational ITC is excluded), while it does include several non-operational UN departments.

As Chair of the UNDG, the Administrator occupies a position that could have been somewhat akin to the earlier envisaged UN director-general. But the mandate is confined only to operations, and within them, mostly concerns process and procedure. Gus Speth and his successors have been willingly acknowledged by other agencies in this role as convenors, but not as coordinators with any influence over the mandates or activities of the respective parts of the system.

Conclusion

Bill Draper was an iconoclastic reformer. He went a long way to modernizing UNDP but, while eschewing UN practices, he succeeded in alienating the rest of the system, which he was known to disdain. Under his successor, UNDP had the task of trying to rebuild some of the broken links.

The HDRs were another watershed, and the capacity for research and knowledge management was an important addition to UNDP's aspiration to become a fully fledged development agency. It had become more of a "program," especially with the creation of a competent cadre of environmental specialists. But almost everywhere outside these new pockets of expertise residing in headquarters, UNDP was still a fund manager, and that role was also growing. Thus UNDP had not become any easier to define. Project management was still the main preoccupation in country offices. It would require a rather different staff profile in the field for UNDP to become predominantly a policy organization. Following Speth, Malloch Brown was to take up the challenge and make it one of his priorities during his six-year tenure.

3 UNDP in the twenty-first century

- A focus on change
- World Bank, poverty, and the MDGs
- Intrusion of politics
- Current size and structure
- Regionalization
- Conclusion

This chapter brings history to the present and describes UNDP in the first decade of the twenty-first century. It traces the contributions and the consequences of the three most recent Administrators, the evolution in the development priorities of the organization, and the current structure, including UNDP's most significant structural change, taking it down the path of regionalization.

A focus on change

In 1999, Speth left UNDP and was replaced by someone who contrasted strongly with all his predecessors. Mark Malloch Brown (United Kingdom) was the first non-US citizen to head UNDP. Before his appointment, Europe had decided that, with US core contributions slipping from the top rank, it was its turn to provide the next Administrator. The EU duly proposed the Danish Minister of Development Cooperation to the Secretary-General, but Kofi Annan turned instead to this World Banker, who he had already known for many years, and who he had asked to work with the UN on a public information strategy.[1] Although he had spent time in the private sector, he was also something of an insider to the system, having cut his development teeth in UNHCR[2] early in his career. He had also known UNDP from the vantage point of its chief development rival.

He had been a political and communications consultant in New York before joining the World Bank, where he became vice-president for external relations, including liaison with the UN. He brought to UNDP a strong belief in the power of advocacy and some formidable communication skills, which were to raise the organization's profile considerably.

From his first day, he set about comprehensively recasting UNDP. The style was very different. Speth had waited until mid-term to set up a process based on elaborate internal consultation ("UNDP 2001"). Malloch Brown started change management in a more literal sense— by changing the managers. Although the process was more protracted than he would have liked, four of the five regional directors (assistant administrators) were replaced within 12 months. He also announced his aim to reduce the number of staff in headquarters by 25 percent, a process begun early but effected over two years.

Consultation was instituted through annual global surveys begun in 2000, an internal one for all staff and one for external partners. The global staff survey gauged levels of satisfaction with the goals of the reform, and was an important barometer of morale. It also provided feedback on the performance of supervisors and of individual offices within the organization, with consequences for the staff concerned. By the fifth round of surveys in 2004, the response rates were high: well over 90 percent of staff (a total of 5,895) responded to the internal survey, and 1,630 to the partners' survey. The trends over the four years showed positive perceptions of the changes.[3]

UNDP was to be given a clearer policy stamp. The Bureau for Development Policy was a key target and a narrowing and deepening process was begun, designed to reflect more accurately the focus areas. Out went some of the programs (and staff) in areas where he considered other UN agencies were pre-eminent, such as health (except HIV/AIDS) (WHO) and forestry (FAO), with half of the 200-plus staff of the Bureau turning over in the first two years. This would have been the opportunity to bring into the Bureau the Human Development Report Office and the Office of Development Studies—two other UNDP entities concerned primarily with research and policy. But the opportunity to pursue further mainstreaming of the human development paradigm was missed, and the three offices have continued their independent existence.

In several key respects, Malloch Brown was fortunate to follow Speth, because his predecessor had laid some solid foundations on which to build. The same program priorities were maintained. Enlarging on the "special development situations" priority, and in recognition of the growing challenges of fragile statehood, he established a full Bureau for Crisis Prevention and Recovery. Questioning the communications appeal of "sustainable human development," (SHD) the "enabling environment for SHD" became democratic governance. To the other priorities of environment and poverty reduction, two more were added, partly as an opportunistic move to attract more funding. One was HIV/AIDS prevention and care; the other was information and communication technologies (ICT).

There was already a unit of HIV/AIDS and Development, which, in contrast to the more epidemiological approaches of other agencies, attempted to highlight the broader economic and social impacts of the pandemic. It was a valid area for UNDP activity in which a growing number of the country offices were working with local NGOs to raise awareness of the consequences of AIDS and address gender and human rights concerns. Then, as funding was ramped up in the Global Fund for AIDS, Tuberculosis and Malaria (GFATM), the UNDP offices in countries with weak institutions became recipients and implementers of assistance. As of 2010, UNDP was managing GFATM grants with a total value of $US1.2 billion in 26 countries.[4]

The designation of ICT as a priority was prompted by the first-ever invitation to a UNDP Administrator to attend a G8 summit in Okinawa, Japan in 2000, in which the development benefits of ICT were highlighted and at which the Japanese government pledged to provide a considerable amount of assistance. The immediate upshot was the creation of the Digital Opportunities Task-force (DOT force) jointly coordinated by UNDP and the World Bank, which provided a report to the following year's G8 meeting in Genoa, Italy. Periodically, the knowledge revolution driven by ICT has been hyped as an opportunity for development organizations to help developing countries use technology to accelerate their progress. UNDP, UNESCO, International Telecommunications Union, and others have helped to raise awareness of the benefits of ICT and funded projects to support local hardware and software development. But, as in many other development domains, it is neither funding nor technical inputs that is lacking, but appropriate national policies. These are much harder to change.[5] Japan put $5 million into a trust fund for UNDP to support ICT projects. But the anticipated large-scale funding from Japan and other donors was not forthcoming and the ICT priority was dropped by UNDP in 2003.

The six priorities (Table 3.1) were designated as practice areas, with their own "communities" within the organization. Again building on an earlier UNDP innovation, these communities (staff with interests in the topics) were linked through email-based knowledge networks, which were each managed by a facilitator. Through these communities, staff could record their experiences and learn from practice elsewhere. For a highly decentralized organization, this knowledge networking has been a powerful means of fostering staff commitment to UNDP's priorities.

Like all his predecessors, Malloch Brown was faced with the challenge of finding UNDP's place in an increasingly crowded and competitive development arena. He knew the UN from his days in UNHCR, and from his long acquaintance with the Secretary-General. He was even more familiar with the World Bank, on behalf of which he had exercised his formidable promotional skills through some difficult periods.[6] UNDP could act as a useful bridge between the UN system and the bank, but it also needed to find its own leadership role.

World Bank, poverty, and the MDGs

Speth had instituted contacts between his regional directors and their opposite numbers in the bank. Early on, Malloch Brown began a series of meetings with the bank's president, Jim Wolfensohn, with whom he had worked closely in his previous job. The most competitive issue was over the bank's new (1999) invention, the Poverty Reduction Strategy Paper (PRSP), which was a basis of conditionality for concessional lending to the poor countries. It thus had to be taken very seriously by the borrowers, and it had the strong support of the bank's major shareholders.

The UN system saw the PRSP as the bank's bid for leadership in poverty reduction. Several years before, in 1995, the UN's World Summit in Copenhagen had recommended the development of comprehensive national poverty reduction strategies, which UNDP and other UN agencies had subsequently helped many developing countries to draw up.[7] But the bank had gone about developing the PRSPs in a rather top-down manner, ignoring its own strictures about full local consultation, in order to meet the objectives of an unrealistic timetable, which subsequently had to be relaxed. Malloch Brown understood, however, that, despite its shortcomings,[8] the PRSP "was the only game in town" because for the poorest countries it was the key to unlocking large-scale debt cancellation and further long-term lending. But he offered UNDP as a partner in the PRSP countries to facilitate local consultative processes, and urged the country offices to assist.

Then, in September 2000, the largest-ever gathering of world leaders (189, of whom 147 were heads of state and government) met at the UN

Table 3.1 UNDP program priorities, 1998–2010

	1998	2000	2002	2004	2006	2008	2010
	Speth	*Malloch Brown*			*Dervis*		*Clark*
Main theme	Sustainable human development (SHD)	Human development			Human development through capacity development	Human development through capacity development	Human development through capacity development
Cross-cutting priorities	HIV/AIDS	Gender					Gender HIV/AIDS
Priorities (practice areas)	Governance (enabling environment for SHD)	Governance	Democratic governance	Democratic governance	Democratic governance	Democratic governance	Democratic governance
	Poverty and sustainable livelihoods	Poverty reduction	Poverty reduction	Poverty reduction	Poverty reduction	Poverty reduction and the MDGs	Poverty reduction and the MDGs
	Environment	Environment	Energy and environment	Energy and environment	Energy and environment	Environment and sustainable development	Environment and sustainable development

Table 3.1 (continued)

	1998	2000	2002	2004	2006	2008	2010
	Speth	*Malloch Brown*			*Dervis*		*Clark*
	Countries in special development situations	Crisis prevention and recovery	Crisis prevention and recovery	Crisis prevention and recovery	Crisis prevention and recovery	Crisis prevention and recovery	Crisis prevention and recovery
	Gender equality	Gender					
		HIV/AIDS	HIV/AIDS	HIV/AIDS	HIV/AIDS		
				ICT			
						Women's empowerment	

Source: Craig N. Murphy, *The United Nations Development Programme: A Better Way?* (Cambridge: Cambridge University Press, 2006), 320; and annual reports of the UNDP administrator.

for the Millennium Summit. Both in size and substance, the conference was historic, and resulted in the Millennium Declaration, signed by every participant. The declaration contained some bold statements and committed the leaders to standards of governance, freedom, equality, tolerance, and human rights. It also incorporated a number of development goals to be achieved by every country by 2015. Most of these goals had been developed in the course of the UN conferences of the previous decade. But the declaration now constituted the most explicit development and anti-poverty agenda ever to be endorsed by the world's leaders. It was an opportunity for the UN system to forge its own response.

Box 3.1 Millennium Development Goals, targets, and indicators

Goal 1: Eradicate extreme poverty and hunger
Targets:

- Halve the proportion of people whose income is less than $1 a day
- Achieve full and productive employment and decent work for all, including women and young people
- Halve, between 1990 and 2015, the proportion of people who suffer from hunger

Goal 2: Achieve universal primary education
Target:

- Ensure that, by 2015, children everywhere, boys and girls alike, will be able to complete a full course of primary schooling

Goal 3: Promote gender equality and empower women
Target:

- Eliminate gender disparity in primary and secondary education, preferably by 2005, and in all levels of education no later than 2015

Goal 4: Reduce child mortality
Target:

- Reduce by two-thirds, between 1990 and 2015, the under-five mortality rate

Goal 5: Improve maternal health

Targets:

- Reduce by three-quarters, between 1990 and 2015, the maternal mortality ratio
- Achieve, by 2015, universal access to reproductive health

Goal 6: Combat HIV/AIDS, malaria, and other diseases

Targets:

- Have halted by 2015, and begun to reverse, the spread of HIV/AIDS
- Achieve, by 2010, universal access to treatment for HIV/AIDS for all those who need it
- Have halted by 2015, and begun to reverse, the incidence of malaria and other major diseases

Goal 7: Ensure environmental sustainability

Targets:

- Integrate the principles of sustainable development into country policies and programs, and reverse the loss of environmental resources
- Reduce biodiversity loss, achieving by 2010 a significant reduction in the rate of loss
- Halve, by 2015, the proportion of the population without sustainable access to safe drinking water and basic sanitation
- By 2020, to have achieved a significant improvement in the lives of at least 100 million slum dwellers

Goal 8: Develop a global partnership for development

Targets:

- Develop further an open, rule-based, predictable, non-discriminatory trading and financial system
- Address the special needs of the least-developed countries (LDCs)
- Deal comprehensively with developing countries' debt
- In cooperation with the private sector, make available the benefits of new technologies, especially information and communications

Source: United Nations, *Millennium Development Goals Report 2010*, www.un.org/millenniumgoals/pdf/MDG%20Report%202010%20En% 20r15%20-low%20res%2020100615%20-.pdf

The UN secretariat played an exemplary role in drafting the declaration, but the subsequent reaction was flat-footed. The declaration was a document of unique authority, which deserved to be disseminated quickly around the globe as an agenda for action. But the UN system and its extensive country network was not mobilized, civil society was not apprised, and the declaration was not even translated into local languages (besides the six of the UN). Only three months later, in December 2000, did the General Assembly agree that a "road map" for implementation of the declaration be drawn up by the UN and submitted to it the following year.

Early in 2001, however, Malloch Brown was one of the first to see the opportunity provided by the declaration. In February, UNDP produced the first country report (Tanzania) on achieving the declaration's "Millennium Development Goals"—the first appearance of the "MDGs"—and proposed to Kofi Annan to become the "scorekeeper and campaign manager" for their achievement. The MDGs were to be the UN's counter-weight to the bank's PRSPs and, in the course of 2001, the goals of the Millennium Declaration were refined into a total of eight, with specific targets and indicators added.

In 2002, Malloch Brown persuaded Jeffrey Sachs, a well-known Harvard economist with a strong record of development advocacy,[9] to become a special adviser to the UN on the MDGs. UNDP facilitated his entry, providing him with resources and office space, and Sachs developed the Millennium Project, comprising task forces of experts in ten different development areas relevant to the MDGs. Sachs' report, *Investing in Development*, was completed in 2005 and among many other recommendations, it proposed that "developing country governments should craft and implement MDG-based poverty reduction strategies in transparent and inclusive processes, working closely with civil society organizations, the domestic private sector and international partners."[10] It was a return to Copenhagen. In countries undertaking PRSPs, the report recommended that the MDGs be incorporated into the strategies.[11]

Also in 2002, the UN held a world conference on development financing in Monterrey, Mexico in which Malloch Brown wanted UNDP to play an influential role. He proposed "a grand bargain" according to which developing countries striving to achieve MDGs 1 to 7 would be supported by developed countries meeting MDG 8: aid for goals. This was the core sentiment of the Monterrey Consensus, which emerged from the meeting.[12]

UNDP's scorekeeping role came to be shared with the UN DESA, which had stronger statistical expertise (although the Human Development

Report Office was developing a large rival database of indicators). But the advocacy role stayed with UNDP, which funded a millennium campaign based in headquarters and encouraged country offices to produce regular reports on MDG achievement.

These reports could—and probably should—have been combined with the national Human Development Reports that most country offices were already producing, especially because the MDGs were essentially indicators of some of the key aspects of human development. But after protracted discussions in New York, and over the objections of many of the country offices, two-track reporting was maintained. On the positive side, however, the growing role of UNDP (and its local partners) in reporting on development status country by country was a means of capitalizing on one of the most important potential strengths of an extensive UN field network.

But UNDP's country offices were under additional strain. They were also included in the comprehensive reforms during the first half of the decade. Core resources were to be cut by 15 percent in the field and each office was to undergo "reprofiling," which meant redefining all the posts and asking staff to reapply. On its own terms, the restructuring was successful. Many staff (mainly local) were shed and the offices were forced to reassess their roles and deploy resources more effectively.

With some exceptions, however—particularly in Latin America and Asia—the country offices have remained the most significant area of UNDP weakness, whereas they are touted as the organization's principal strength. As discussed in Chapter 4, the offices are multi-layered and top-heavy. The quality of their international staff is highly uneven. Few offices are headed by genuine development specialists (particularly as compared with the World Bank offices in the same countries) with the knowledge and the confidence to act as authoritative policy and program advisers. In many cases, also, the administrative, financial, and other services that country offices provide—in particular to fellow UN agencies, which are charged for them—are poor. The fact that there are some notable exceptions to the majority is scarcely reassuring. It demonstrates that higher standards are achievable but not generalized, and highlights the difficulties UNDP has faced during the latter part of its history of fragmentation and non-uniformity across regions and among its bureaus.

Every UNDP administration has needed to define its position within the UN development system. Bill Draper sought distance from the UN by almost severing the long-standing funding links and rebranding the organization as "World Development" with a new (green) logo. Gus Speth retained the logo, but restored links with the system through the

UN Development Group. Malloch Brown took UNDP through a new branding exercise designed to shore up its UN identity. The old logo was replaced with the blue UN emblem and the organization was now described as the system's development network.

UNDP had by this time become a larger organization, but with a more distinctive program profile. During the 2000s, UNDP's resources were growing steadily, from $US2.4 billion in 2000 to $US3.8 billion in 2004.[13] Although there was a revival in multilateral resources (i.e. to the core budget), growth was much faster in targeted (non-core) contributions, both from developed and developing countries. During the four-year period 2004–07, annual average expenditures were over $US3.5 billion (Table 3.2), of which a significant portion was for staff. Additional funding empowered UNDP as an organization of increasing program substance, but by funding its own activities, it had lost the influence it had had when it had been the principal funder of other UN agencies and organizations.[14] So from here on, its relationship with the system was no longer central, but parallel in nature. The refinement of the programming mandate to concentrate more on the areas not covered by other parts of the system—particularly in governance, energy, and crisis prevention—underlined this new parallelism, although there were still some areas (such as international trade and private-sector development) where UNDP overlapped with other more experienced UN agencies.

This parallelism, however, made cooperation within the system harder to achieve, particularly because UNDP was in competition with other UN entities for some of the same sources of funding. The credibility of UNDP's second role as "coordinator" of the rest of the system was consequently under strain, and called for a firewalling of its

Table 3.2 UNDP expenditures on program priorities, 2004–2009

Priority (practice) area	2004–2007 (annual average)	2008	2009
Poverty reduction and achievement of MDGs	926	1,255	1,175
Democratic governance	1,295	1,429	1,473
Crisis prevention and recovery	392	657	610
Environment and sustainable development	316	404	505
Other (including inter-country programs)	644*	352	343
Total	3,573	4,097	4,108

* includes inter-country resources in above priority areas
Source: UNDP Annual Report 2008

program activities. UNDP's response in the field, where most of its work is undertaken, has been to appoint its own country directors in its largest offices, leaving the UN resident coordinator—previously also the UNDP head—to concentrate exclusively on system-wide responsibilities.

Intrusion of politics

Even before he joined UNDP, Malloch Brown's communications skills had been called upon by Kofi Annan. At the end of 2004, in the midst of the Iraq oil-for-food imbroglio, he was called again across First Avenue, initially to become *Chef de Cabinet* concurrently with his UNDP job and, in mid-2005, the full-time UN Deputy Secretary-General for the remainder of Annan's term.

For the first time, there was a global competition for the Administrator's post and it was won by Kemal Derviş of Turkey, who took up the position in August 2005. He brought an outstanding development CV to the position. He had also had a successful career in the World Bank, holding the vice-presidency successively for the Middle East region and for the Poverty Reduction and Economic Management department. Before joining UNDP, he had been recalled to Turkey in 2001 as Minister of Finance to help see the country through its economic crisis, subsequently becoming a member of the Turkish parliament and chief negotiator on EU accession.

Derviş spoke more languages (four) and knew more economics (and development economists) than any of his predecessors, and he was therefore well-matched with the original, more cerebral aspirations of UNDP, which early pioneers such as I.G. Patel and Arthur Lewis had wished for. He was no less committed to reform than Malloch Brown, but his vision was even broader and more idealistic, encompassing the UN system as a whole. Central to his thinking was the revived proposal for a UN Economic and Social Security Council (UNESC),[15] which he described in the book he published just before joining UNDP.[16]

The UNESC would be the governance umbrella for all specialized economic and social agencies currently in the UN system, such as the ILO, UNDP, UNCTAD, etc., as well as the Bretton Woods institutions and the WTO. The job of the UNESC would be to provide an overall framework of coherence and efficiency to international institutions and cooperation in the economic and social spheres. Derviş's UNESC was an Economic and Social Council (ECOSOC) with sharpened teeth. It would have very high-level country membership and—while not side-stepping the governance arrangements of each individual agency—it would have the authority to appoint the heads of all the UN entities, World Bank, IMF, and WTO, reviewing performance and effectiveness, and helping to mobilize resources.

Derviş did become involved in UN reform, but not on the scale of his own vision. In 2006, a High-level Panel on System-wide Coherence— set up largely at the instigation of Malloch Brown in his new role as UN Deputy Secretary-General—published its report.[17] The recommendations had the authority of the three heads of governments who chaired it (Mozambique, Norway, and Pakistan), and a membership that included two former heads of state (Chile and Tanzania) as well as Kemal Derviş in *ex officio* capacity. Given the time available to the Panel, which had to report within a year and before the expiry of Kofi Annan's term, its proposals were not all that radical, and they were diluted further by a conservative General Assembly. However, the premises of "Delivering as One" were retained, and of particular concern to UNDP was the forging of closer programming and funding relations among UN entities at the field level: "the establishment of One United Nations at the country level, with one leader, one programme, one budget and, where appropriate, one office."[18] The proposal became known as the Four Ones.

While the "first UN" (governments) were reluctant reformers, the "second UN" (agency staff) were scarcely more open to change.[19] Initially, eight pilot countries were identified to deliver as one, but there was little initial enthusiasm among the representatives of the specialized agencies, and the reforms proceeded through the UN Development Group with less than a whole-hearted consensus. Greater convergence at country level was, however, welcomed by some of the major donors, and the establishment of one-UN funds helped to catalyze the process. Derviş played an important part in this potentially significant reform measure.

As Administrator, however, his impact was more muted. While he retained this big-picture mentality throughout his relatively short tenure, it must be assumed that aspects of the administrator's job— inevitably weighted with the more prosaic tasks of managing a global operation of 6,000 dispersed staff—held limited appeal. In 2006, the Dutch politician (and former leader of the Labor Party) Ad Melkert was appointed as associate administrator. He had been a candidate for the top job, but he seemed a fortuitous choice as deputy because Derviş came to rely on him to oversee the day-to-day running of UNDP.[20]

The funding situation in UNDP remained sound. In December 2006, the Spanish government announced the creation of the "MDG

Achievement Fund" and provided over US$700 through UNDP to finance projects in 59 countries of bilateral interest to the donor. UNDP set up a separate office to run the program, which was intended for implementation through agencies and organizations of the UN system.[21] By 2010, projects had been formulated in 49 countries, involving 20 UN agencies and organizations. UNDP's share as implementer was over one quarter.[22]

Core funding also progressed, and in 2008 it again topped US$1 billion. By now, however, this source, still subscribed almost exclusively by developed country donors, represented less than one-fifth of UNDP's total resources, which had now risen to over US$5 billion (program and non-program). The MDG Achievement Fund was an example of the "bilateral donor resources," which had become a larger component of income. The largest share in 2009 was being taken by "multilateral donor resources," including the European Commission, the regional development banks, and the Global Environment Facility. The fourth component of funding comprised the contributions of program countries, particularly in Latin America. The fifth type of income included contributions to UNDP's own subsidiary organizations: UNIFEM, UNV, and UNCDF (Figure 3.1).

The resources profile reflected a healthy funding situation, but also revealed the type of organization which UNDP had become. The *raison d'être* had always been as a UN fund. But in the 1990s, it had largely abandoned its role as funder of other UN entities. While it had had some recent success in attracting funds, which it managed on behalf of the system—the pooled ("One UN") funds for individual countries, for example, or the MDG Achievement Fund—these fund-management activities were increasingly firewalled off from the rest of UNDP, mostly into the Multi-donor Trust Fund Office, acting as a conduit and earning overhead fees. These funding operations were in parallel. Other funds which UNDP attracted were for itself, because over the years the organization had steadily built up its own capacity as an implementing agency.

As this bifurcation developed, UNDP was increasingly motivated by resource mobilization. The capacity to raise money was a primary— and, in the eyes of some managers, the most important—success criterion by which staff and offices were evaluated. Collisions with the rest of the system were inevitable. In the first place, even with some careful circumvention, new funding opportunities lead to mission creep, with inevitable duplication of activities with other agencies. In the second place, UNDP competed actively with the rest of the system on the doorsteps of the same donors and funding sources.[23]

Derviş's term was not untroubled, however. In early 2007, a few months after the Democratic People's Republic of Korea (DPRK) had attracted the world's opprobrium in testing a nuclear weapon, the US mission to the UN in New York made some serious allegations about UNDP's activities in the country. The ambassador sent a letter to Ad Melkert accusing UNDP of complicity with a dictatorship, maintaining that the country office was in violation of UN rules, and a source of hard currency and other resources with no assurance that they were utilized for legitimate development activities.[24]

Given the general hostility of the Bush Administration towards the UN at the time, the US *démarche* was part political opportunism. The

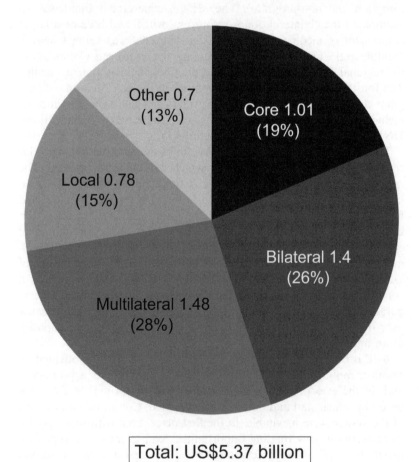

Figure 3.1 Sources of UNDP funding, 2009 (US$ billion)

accusations could have been reversed, since the United States has always been a conscientious governor of the UN and a member of the 2005 UNDP Executive Board, which approved the country program for DPRK. However, there is a broader concern behind these accusations, which is why it merits attention.

The DPRK country office of UNDP (as well as UNICEF, WFP, and others) was long-established, but it had always operated differently from nearly every other. The local Korean staff were not recruited according to merit, but nominated by the government. There was limited transparency in the manner in which the government—as the exclusive national partner—utilized the resources it received from UNDP, and the international staff were restricted in their movements within the country. As even some UNDP insiders had been asking over many years: why was UNDP operating in a country under conditions that so clearly abrogated UN principles? While it might be important to maintain a UN presence to facilitate contacts with the government, did this merit a fully fledged country office and program headed by an official at an elevated rank? At the least, a continuing presence oblivious to the unfolding security crisis showed gross political *naiveté* by the UN's foremost "democratic governance" organization. UNDP responded to the accusations, but failed to convince the critics. It agreed that personnel practices "did not follow worldwide UNDP staffing rules"[25] and was judged to be slow in opening its books on the Korean operations.[26]

A more parochial crisis blew up in the same year, which also impugned the senior management. As a successor to the Multi-Year Funding Framework (MYFF), which acted as the main program budget instrument, UNDP prepared a Strategic Plan for 2008–11 and presented it for approval to the Executive Board in January 2007. While the plan was welcomed in principle, delegations found fault with many aspects of it. Among other things, they wanted more analysis of lessons learnt from the MYFF, and clearer goals and indicators; they found the format at odds with the frameworks of sister organizations such as UNICEF and UNFPA; they saw overlap with the activities of other UN organizations.[27] Following the January session, intensive consultations were initiated with delegations to make it more acceptable. A revised version was debated in September 2007 and endorsed, but only under strict conditions that further changes would be forthcoming. A final version was not formally signed off until the annual session of the Board in June 2008.

The plan was important because it was the formal basis for spending authorizations. The delays in approval meant disruptions to the continuity of operations, and added uncertainty for staff whose contracts depended on the Plan's approval. The fate of a single document need not in itself have been grounds for a crisis, but the matter was poorly managed by UNDP. The Administrator's absence from key sessions of the Board[28] also added to concerns in the Executive Board about his commitment to the organization.

It also became known that, for much of his tenure, Derviş had based his home in Washington, travelling to New York during weekdays. It was apparent to UNDP staff that his heart had never really left Washington, where he had spent more than 20 years. He was not the first top-flight economist to join UNDP, but like I.G. Patel, Arthur Lewis, and others, he probably found insufficient substance in UNDP to satisfy his redoubtable intellectual strengths. UNDP certainly had some sound development specialists, but—intellectually speaking—a general comparison of UNDP professional staff with his former colleagues in the World Bank would have been unfavorable. The main exceptions were to be found in and around the Human Development Report Office (which had attracted former World Bank staff), but it has remained out of the mainstream of UNDP's operations. When Kemal Derviş announced his resignation in early 2009, several months before the end of his four-year contract, it was to return to Washington, where he took up an appointment with the Brookings Foundation. There was an unfortunate irony in the fact that the first UNDP Administrator to have been chosen on a meritocratic basis, and with the strongest resumé of any of his predecessors, had been so short-lived.

Derviş's departure left Ad Melkert in charge, but only briefly. He was again a leading candidate for the top job, for which he would have been fully qualified in the light of his experience, but the baton passed to someone from an entirely new continent. Helen Clark arrived in April 2009, having recently left her post as Prime Minister of New Zealand, a position she had held for nine years. A few months later, Melkert was appointed UN special representative for Iraq, and Rebeca Grynspan, already a UNDP regional director and a former Vice-President of Costa Rica, was appointed as associate administrator.

For the first time, there were not one but two women heading UNDP, reflecting a trend at the top of the UN organization, where women now occupy the majority of the senior positions.[29] Each brought a background of politics into their position, which, given the recent strains in the relationship between the board and the secretariat, has proved to be important. Aside from restoring good relations with her governors, Helen Clark has soon established herself with staff as a sensitive and approachable manager, helping to improve morale in

UNDP at a time when its role within the UN system continues to be a matter of speculation.

Unlike some of her predecessors, Helen Clark has not wanted to shake the organizational tree with more reforms. Rather, her intention is to build on what she has found. She sees no difficulty with UNDP's dual roles of development agency and system coordinator. Indeed, she feels it "critical that UNDP is a substantive agency" and that resident coordinators have funds at their disposal. This is true to the *primus inter pares* principle, but is as far as ever from the original concept of UNDP as the central funding and coordination body.[30]

Thematically, Clark intends her hallmark to be "the integration of the poverty and environment agendas," with governance as the "precursor" (author's conversation with Helen Clark, 18 November 2010). Perhaps inadvertently, she has rather precisely espoused Gustave Speth's sustainable human development paradigm of the 1990s, which was complemented by the "enabling environment" (later to be known as democratic governance). The main difference, however, is the emphasis she places on climate change, which, as one of the signatories of the 2000 Millennium Declaration, she claims was not adequately taken into account by the MDGs. Helen Clark has made the achievement of the MDGs a key focus of UNDP—tagging them with poverty as one of the four practice areas—as well as of the UN development system through her role as chair of the UN development group.

Current size and structure

Today, UNDP is an organization of nearly 7,000 people, about the same staff size as the UN High Commission for Refugees (UNHCR) and about one-third smaller than UNICEF and the WFP.[31] These four main field-based agencies of the UN together employ over 30,000 staff.

Of the UNDP total, some 3,000 (42 percent) are professional and the remainder are support staff. A total of 1,200 staff are in New York, with more than four times that number serving in the 130 country and liaison offices and the regional service centers. Most of the staff belong to one or other of nine separate bureaux, each headed by an assistant secretary-general: five regional bureaux, the Partnerships Bureau, the Bureau for Development Policy, the Bureau for Crisis Prevention and Recovery, and the Bureau of Management. There are also three subsidiary organizations: UNIFEM and UNCDF, both in New York, and the UNV in Bonn, Germany. UNIFEM is scheduled to be phased out in 2011 following the creation of UN Women, a new entity proposed by the UN reform program of 2006, unifying the other main UN bodies concerned with gender affairs. In her UNDP role, the Administrator has reporting directly to her the Human Development Report Office, Evaluation Office, Office of Audit and Investigation, and Ethics Office. The UN Development Operations Coordination Office reports to her in her role as Chair of the UNDG, comprising nearly all the operational entities of the UN (Figure 3.2).

Over the past 20 years, there have been additions to the overall structure of UNDP, reflecting the organization's adaptation to opportunities. In 1990, the human development report office was established on separate premises to assuage concerns about its independence. But it has remained fully funded by UNDP. UNDP has had a presence in Europe for many years, with offices in Bulgaria, Cyprus, Poland, Romania, and Turkey, as well as Switzerland (Geneva) for liaison purposes. Soon after the break-up of the Soviet Union in 1991, the division for eastern Europe was enlarged and it was subsequently upgraded to a full bureau as the number of offices grew. In 1996, the rather eccentric decision was taken by the then regional director to open an office in Slovakia (Bratislava) as a regional center, just next door to the large UN center in Vienna. With the enlargement of the European Union, the number of offices has declined, but the importance of some—especially in Central Asia and the Caucusus—has increased.

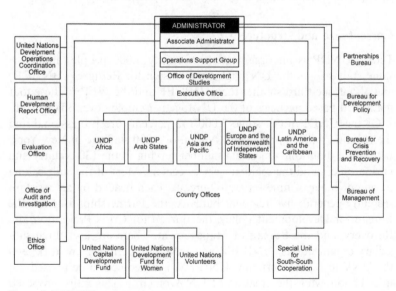

Figure 3.2 UNDP structure

Also during the 1990s, a division for "conflict-affected" countries was enlarged to a full Bureau for Crisis Prevention and Recovery (BCPR) as the opportunities for funding post-conflict and natural disaster recovery came UNDP's way. The UN has never managed the humanitarian-to-development transition very well, but it was an area where UNDP's country presence and breadth of mandate gave it an advantage. The creation of the bureau required some in-house realignments. Countries with major recovery programs—such as Rwanda in the 1990s; Afghanistan and Iraq in the 2000s—became the joint responsibility of BCPR and the relevant regional bureau. But the demarcations of responsibility were not always clear. Conflict prevention and recovery also became one of the main practice areas of UNDP, but under the responsibility of the bureau, and not—like the other practice areas—under the Bureau for Development Policy (BDP). Yet there were clear overlaps between governance (BDP) and conflict prevention (BCPR), which have not been fully resolved.

In every development organization, there are always tensions between geography and substance, often leading to repeated restructuring. In the World Bank, the departments dealing with substantive development domains were traditionally predominant, but the geographic departments gained more prominence as the bank devolved more staff and authority to its country offices. In UNDP it was the other way round: the countries, their resident representatives, and their bureaux were always the real drivers of the organization. But over the past 20 years, UNDP has strengthened its own areas of expertise, initially all concentrated in New York, but with the practice areas gradually reaching out to the country offices. BDP's expanding role in development policy was at first resented by the regional bureaux, some of which began to recruit their own policy advisers rather than relying on the expertise of BDP. The creation of a network of regional service centers enabled policy advisory services, in support of country offices, to be managed jointly by the regional bureau and BDP. The ensuing regionalization process was the most comprehensive change in UNDP's structure since its inception, and it merits more detailed attention both because of the change and because of the problems of organizational coherence which the process has highlighted.

Regionalization

Until recently, UNDP had never had a decentralized regional structure. But it has always had powerful regional bureaux, located in New York headquarters, from where the oversight of the country offices was provided. The strength of the regional bureaux derives from the seniority of the directors (assistant secretary-generals), whose provenance has always been from their respective regions, and from the authority they exert over their country offices. The directors always have to approve—and very often propose—the appointments of the heads of the offices (UNDP resident representatives/UN resident coordinators and country directors), and they evaluate their performance annually. The country offices therefore feel that they are working for the regional bureaux as much as for the organization as a whole, and there is a strong sense of loyalty, underscored by the fact that in today's UNDP the heads of the country offices are also usually from the same region.

The independence of the regional bureaux has periodically caused headaches for UNDP administrators wishing to promulgate organization-wide policies and practices; regional directors have always been able to count on their own constituency of country office heads to maintain their autonomy. This feature of the structure of UNDP—more than any other—explains the weak corporate cohesion that has always characterized the organization, with its highly decentralized operations. The local customization of its programming is an undoubted strength, but it inevitably results in a dilution of identity and a lack of uniformity in the conduct of its operations. This lack of uniformity has been nowhere more apparent than in the approach to regionalization, both in substance and in form.

Substance

The regional bureaux have always funded and managed regional projects, which have had broadly three kinds of objective: first, fostering inter-country cooperation, designed to bring countries together around common problems; second, creating regional public goods, such as the production of regional HDRs (of which the Arab HDR is the best example); and third, administering multi-country projects that provide similar advice and services to several countries at a time. The rationale for the first type of project is provided by the advantages of joint management of natural resources (e.g. river basins benefiting several states) or other cross-border exchanges (e.g. regional monetary and trade agreements). The rationale for the second and third types of regional project is often economies of scale.

Traditionally, the regional bureaux provided funding for regional projects through the respective UN regional commissions and the other executing agencies of the UN development system. The content of these projects, and the complexion of these respective regional programs, were determined in a largely *ad hoc* manner, and were the result of the nature of the dialogue each respective regional bureau conducted with the corresponding regional commission, the agencies, and the governments. By their very nature, regional (and all supra-national) projects do not result from the same clarity of mandate as country projects, because there is not a single "*demandeur*." For this reason, an external agent has a privileged vantage point compared with governments, which—while they can benefit from inter-country initiatives—are naturally more preoccupied with national than inter-country concerns. The role of an external sponsor such as UNDP thus becomes significant in helping to inspire and catalyze regional cooperation. And having a large network of offices means that UNDP is well positioned to help countries both to bring their national interests to bear on regional initiatives, and to derive national benefits from cooperation.[32]

As UNDP's links with its traditional executing agencies became looser in the 1990s, this *ex cathedra* role became even more important, especially as UNDP chose not to rely on the UN's own regional commissions to identify regional cooperation opportunities. Yet, while it would not have been hard to do, UNDP has never provided a clear statement of the specific advantages which it can claim as a sponsor of regional cooperation in its various forms, and has no clear organization-wide policy. This absence of an organizational vision and understanding of its role as a promoter of regional cooperation helps to explain the highly variegated profiles of regional programming in UNDP, both over time and between regional bureaux. Significant variations of substance between regions would be expected because of different regional development circumstances and needs. But even the approaches and modalities in the use of regional funds have been *ad hoc* and expedient, often reflecting the specific proclivities of the regional directors for whom these programs were a valuable source of patronage.

Form

From the earliest years, UNDP has debated whether it needed a regional structure. In the 1960s, Robert Jackson had anticipated an eventual merger, even an absorption, of the UN regional commissions by the regional bureaux.[33] But, notwithstanding the evidently valuable role UNDP has played as a sponsor of regional initiatives, the rationale for a meso-level between headquarters and the country offices has never been convincing. Firstly, establishing a third structural level is expensive and bureaucratically cumbersome for an organization that already faces criticism for the size and weight of its large country office network (see Chapter 4). Secondly, designated country offices have already taken on *de facto* regional responsibilities in acting as liaison channels with the UN regional commissions, as well as the secretariats of the major sub-regional commissions such as the Association of South-East Asian Nations (ASEAN) in Jakarta, or the Economic Community of West African States (ECOWAS) in Abuja.

However, as part of the "UNDP 2001" change-management process, UNDP decided to build a regional structure, starting in 1997 with the creation of "sub-regional resource facilities" (SuRFs). The SuRFs consisted of clusters of policy advisers outposted from the Bureau for Development Policy, and the intention was to provide backstopping services to country offices in the same sub-regions. The first to be established were in Asia (Bangkok and Islamabad), and in each case they were attached to the respective country offices. Given the individualistic nature of the regional bureaux, however, and in the absence of a clear corporate strategy, regionalization proceeded in a piecemeal fashion, with much trial and error. The Latin America and Arab States bureaux stayed aloof for several years, while Asia and Africa made several changes to their SuRF locations: Addis Ababa was moved to Johannesburg; Islamabad was moved first to Kathmandu, then to Colombo (eschewing for seemingly political reasons the most logical choice, Delhi). When the Arab States bureau agreed to a SuRF, it was established first in Beirut, but then shifted to Cairo. Only Bangkok and Bratislava stayed put, although the latter choice was not based on any clear logic, since there was no country office in Slovakia.

The confusion and the expense only grew when it was decided to start converting SuRFs to "regional service centers," adding more staff and expanding the functions. On this scale, these regional entities began to outgrow their country-office hosts, so in Thailand, Sri Lanka, South Africa, and Lebanon, there were now two UNDP offices—and two office heads—in the capitals. In some regions, there were also sub-centers for particular sub-regions: Suva (Fiji) for the Pacific; Dakar (Senegal) for West Africa; Port of Spain (Trinidad) for the Caribbean. The Asia region sowed its own particular brand of confusion in dividing responsibility between Bangkok and Colombo, not by geography (the original logic), but by practice area, so the offices of the region had to call for support from different centers. The scope of each regional center varied in other ways. Their rationale was essentially based on the third type of regional program (see above), multi-country services, albeit mainly through the funding of new UNDP staff. In some cases, the regional centers took on responsibility for some of the other types of regional program; in some cases not.

Only in 2008 did UNDP produce a comprehensive policy paper on regionalization,[34] in an attempt to bring some order to the evolving process. The definitive locations of the service centers and sub-centers were decided (although the future of Colombo was still in doubt in late 2010) (Table 3.3), but the precise scope and functions of the centers need further clarification.

Table 3.3 also shows the location of the UN regional commissions and other major regional centers of the UN development system. It is apparent that, when UNDP's regional directors decided on the locations of the SuRFs and regional service centers, they took little account of the locations of the long pre-existing UN regional commissions and other UN centers. In fact, regional (and country) locations have always been decided largely autonomously by every part of the UN development system, which explains the growing proliferation of UN regional hubs (there are regional or sub-regional UN offices in a total of 31 cities other than those of the regional commissions[35]).

Belatedly, the UN system has decided to try to bring greater coherence to regional programming, an important frontier not hitherto breached, but the task is complicated by the UN's many regional locations. In Africa alone, there are UN regional offices in 11 different capital cities. To add to the complexity, there are parallel mechanisms designed to improve regional coherence. On one hand, the executive secretaries of the regional commissions (who, as under-secretary-generals, hold the most senior UN positions in each of the five UN regions) convene regular meetings—"regional coordination mechanisms (RCM)"—of

Table 3.3 Locations of UNDP and UN regional centers

	Africa	Asia-Pacific	Latin America	Arab States	Europe
UNDP regional centers	Johannesburg	Bangkok	Panama	Cairo	Bratislava
Sub-centers	Dakar	Colombo, Suva	Port of Spain	–	–
UN regional commission	Addis Ababa	Bangkok	Santiago	Beirut	Geneva
Other major UN centers	Nairobi	New Delhi	Mexico	Amman	Vienna

UN agencies in their respective regions "with a view to improving coordination among the work programs of the organizations of the United Nations system."[36] On the other hand, the regional directors of UNDP convene "regional director teams (RDT)" in order to coordinate better the support of the agencies to the UN country teams of each region. The existence of the two mechanisms reflects the somewhat curious distinction in the UN between what is called "economic and social" and what is called "developmental" or operational. In practice, the RCMs are concerned more with the analysis of regional issues and policies, while the RDTs are focused more on the practical aspects of delivering TA. But the existence of these two types of regional coordination—involving some of the same people coming from a variety of locations—is another consequence of the complicated architecture of the UN development system.

Conclusion

The reforms begun in UNDP at the end of the previous decade were built upon in the first years of the new millennium, and bore fruit. After a temporary loss of momentum, UNDP is today larger and stronger than it has ever been, and it is now under sound new management.

But while UNDP continues to enjoy the confidence of its major donors and its program countries, the amplitude of each wave of reform also signifies that it is still uncertain of its role. UNDP bears little resemblance to the central TA fund of the UN, which was its original rationale. It is still strongly driven by fund mobilization, but now mainly for itself as a fully fledged development agency. In consequence, UNDP's relationship with the rest of the system, which it had once aspired to lead, has also fundamentally changed. As an organization trying to look both inwards and outwards simultaneously—even within the steadily diminishing space occupied by the UN development system—there are inevitable frictions. The ongoing process of regionalization has been symptomatic of these problems. Parochialism still prevails within UNDP, and its instincts as a (not fully cohesive) development agency are not well attuned to its aspirations to continue playing a coordinating role within the UN development system.

Chapter 4 examines in more depth UNDP's performance in both its roles: as development organization and as system coordinator.

4   Performance and results

- **Relevance: one organization, two roles**
- **Effectiveness**
- **Efficiency**
- **Conclusion**

It would be over-ambitious to try to summarize in a single chapter the performance and results of an organization—still less a system of agencies—over several decades. The task is all the more challenging because UNDP, as an institution of process and dialogue, cannot easily highlight milestones of achievement that are both measurable and attributable, as WHO can with disease eradication, or UNICEF with child vaccinations. Indeed, UNDP is rather difficult to define as a development entity, not just because of its amalgam of roles, but because it has no readily definable target constituency.[1] Successive organizational mission statements, following frequent internal reform processes, reveal how UNDP's own image of itself has evolved: from a central funding mechanism, to a human development organization, to today's "global development network [...] advocating for change and connecting countries to knowledge, experience and resources to help people build a better life."[2]

This evolution is also a sign of insecurity. From its postwar antecedents as principal UN funding agency for TA, its rationale as a functional international organization was as a public good—anticipated by President Truman—in helping to transfer know-how from North to South. This role was predicated on a significant and sustained flow of funds, and strong organic links to the technical agencies and organizations of the UN system. For reasons examined by this book, neither condition prevailed. And even if they had, the primacy of UN TA was destined to erode.

This chapter traces how UNDP, once deprived of its original rationale, has pursued dual functions, and examines its relevance, effectiveness, and organizational efficiency in each role.

Relevance: one organization, two roles

The first measure—relevance—is immediately troublesome. All the entities of the UN development system were established to answer specific development needs, in specific sectors and domains, and often in order to draw up and promulgate standards. UNDP, on the other hand, was not so much an organization as an amalgam of two funding facilities, the "need" for which was based on the concern at the time to facilitate the transfer of technical skills from North to South. It was placed at the center of the already established system of UN specialist entities as the main financial motor for TA. Robert Jackson and others soon realized that the UN development system needed a more integrated structure, with UNDP—or something resembling it—at the center (Chapter 1). When no coherent structure materialized, UNDP remained a somewhat disembodied funding facility with a growing global network of offices serving the UN—rather like a postal banking system. But it was held together through the funding that UNDP was able to attract and disburse through the rest of the system.

Then both UNDP and the UN executing agencies, with which it had conscientiously nurtured its contractual relationships, understood that mutual independence was not inevitable: that UNDP could execute its own projects through non-UN channels, and that the agencies could go directly to UNDP's own donors for funding. Quite early in its existence, therefore, UNDP lost its *raison d'être* as a central funding organization.

As it assumed substantive responsibilities—becoming more of a program in the true sense—UNDP started to resemble a microcosm of the UN development system itself, rivaling some of the specialized agencies and programs in their own fields and moving UNDP even further out from the center of the system, which it had once aspired to lead. Then, in a subsequent phase, it has endeavored to move inwards again in pioneering an inspirational UN development paradigm—human development—and narrowing its own specializations in an attempt to locate its own exclusive niches. As a leading idea, UNDP's concept of human development prevailed in the 1990s and gave the organization a sense of focus. But it never became an effective operational guidepost, either for UNDP or for the system. In today's UNDP, its influence is maintained through the annual global Human Development Reports and their country rankings, and the many country reports which are periodic local appraisals of development challenges.

UNDP's centrality at the country level has also ebbed and flowed. The field network preceded the formal foundation of UNDP, and operationally this network has been its main defining feature. UNDP country coordination was facilitated by the fact that its resident representatives were also the local heads of the WFP and the UNFPA, while FAO and UNIDO assigned senior advisers to the offices. Then, as agencies became more financially independent and their own networks proliferated, these and other UN agencies and organizations appointed their own country representatives. In 1977, the General Assembly passed a landmark resolution to implement the findings of a committee that had been set up to restructure the economic and social sectors of the UN (referred to in Chapter 1), which led to the designation of nearly all UNDP's resident representatives as concurrent UN resident coordinators. The proposal was in reaction to the perceived lack of coherence among UN programs within the same country. But, as discussed earlier, by giving two jobs to one person, the proposal raised legitimate concerns among the agencies that UNDP and its programs would be given undue prominence in UN-wide initiatives.

UNDP's search for a role has not been without ambiguity, the signs of which were visible in the early days. The real strength of the field network is to keep the organization's ear to the ground, identifying the specific development priorities of each country. But while these highly differentiated needs are fed upwards, the organization has developed a set of centrally determined development priorities which it attempts to propagate downwards. One recent observer has characterized this tension as UNDP's "riding two horses simultaneously."[3] A 2007 evaluation of results-based management (RBM) in UNDP had made a similar point. While the report determined that RBM had contributed little to development effectiveness at country level, it also found that "reporting against centrally defined outcomes tends to undermine the UNDP's responsiveness and alignment to nationally defined outcomes and priorities."[4]

Of the two roles, the former is legitimate for an organization acting primarily as system coordinator; the latter for a development organization with its own more limited specializations. Today, UNDP is both. It has successfully kept control of the UN resident coordinator network, on which it expends a lot of its own resources, and it has also become a significant development player within the system in such domains as governance and the environment. But the concern that UNDP has become two organizations running in parallel has led to growing calls for it to construct a firewall between its two functions.

Effectiveness

UNDP's effectiveness is linked to the relevance and nature of its role, recognizing that it has in practice followed two tracks: that of development organization on one hand, and of system coordinator on the other.

The development organization

Although UNDP's financial resources have doubled from 2000 to 2010, much of the increase represents a rechanneling, rather than a new mobilization, of funds. "New" funding from the Organization for Economic Cooperation and Development (OECD) countries to UNDP represents a little over 3 percent of their multilateral contributions (2008 figure) and less than 1 percent of their total official development assistance (ODA).[5] Spread over 130 countries (and global and regional programs), the financial footprint of UNDP on the ground is modest, and is dwarfed in most countries by bilateral and other multilateral channels—notably the World Bank, regional development banks, and the European Commission—even in terms of TA grant value. As a development organization, therefore, UNDP, with its highly dispersed constituency of target beneficiaries (unlike, say, the UN specialized agencies or UNICEF), needs to be able to connect with and influence countries in special ways. With certain countries, at different times, when UNDP was a sole or principal player, it has indeed played a key role. Examples are China and Vietnam in the 1980s, Iran and Rwanda in the 1990s, and Afghanistan, Iraq, as well as some small island states in the 2000s. In most countries, however, UNDP's impact as a force for change has waned over the years.

More specifically, the results of its assistance can be judged by the impact of individual projects, whether global, regional, or country. From being an organization that was all things to all countries, often content to fill niches that other donors had left open, UNDP has spent a good part of its life steadily narrowing down the areas of its responsibility, as well as reducing the huge number of its projects, which—notoriously—it has not until very recently been able to track and record centrally. There is not the scope here to attempt to provide an overview of the results of tens of thousands of projects over many years. However, it is possible to impart a sense of effectiveness with respect to the major areas of priority. Each new administrator, starting with Bill Draper in the 1980s, set their own stamp on the organization. At the end of the 1990s, Malloch Brown consolidated all activities around six "practice areas," and moved UNDP out of some areas that belonged more properly to the specialized agencies (detailed in Chapter 3). These six priority areas were subsequently reduced to four (Box 4.1). While the importance of some activities has risen or fallen, the overall program profile has changed little over the past decade.

Poverty reduction and MDG achievement

In 1990, the publication of UNDP's first HDR coincided with the World Bank's most recent World Development Report on poverty.[6] Inevitably, the two reports were compared, and the general consensus was that the HDR came off best, with human development adding essential non-income dimensions to measures of welfare which have come to influence the poverty debate. In subsequent HDRs, UNDP has refined its concept of poverty further (e.g. with a Human Poverty Index) and has therefore continued to play a useful normative function.

In operational terms, however, there has been more limited impact. Following the 1995 World Summit on Social Development in Copenhagen, UNDP had assisted several countries to develop poverty reduction strategies. Some were comprehensive documents and all helped to raise levels of concern with policy-makers. But poverty reduction never became the real driving force of country programming. As UNICEF's historian, a close observer of UNDP, said recently: "In many countries, UNDP programs have mostly been unconnected to any real poverty eradication agenda and contact with the lives of people in the predicament it was supposed to address has been negligible."[7]

In 1999, the World Bank entered the field with its PRSPs, which, although hastily conceived and implemented,[8] framed the conditions for debt alleviation and future concessional lending, and therefore carried considerably more weight with the low-income countries for which they were intended. The PRSP campaign was accompanied by the compilation of an encyclopedic "source book," and the bank went on to develop a considerable body of analysis and guidelines on poverty, including an impressive survey of 60,000 respondents from 60 countries, which resulted in a substantial three-volume study: *Voices of the Poor.*[9]

UNDP could not match the resources of the bank in this area. After the 2000 Millennium Summit, however, Malloch Brown's bargain with the bank was to agree to provide local assistance to their PRSP campaign and ask for its support to the UN in its MDG campaign. It has not quite worked out that way, but UNDP has succeeded in raising the profile of the MDGs as planning targets for countries, producing periodic status reports. Poverty has now been bracketed with the MDGs as a practice area.

Box 4.1 Main priority (practice) areas and focus of activities, 2010

Achieving the MDGs and reducing human poverty

- Promoting inclusive growth, gender equality and MDG achievement
- Fostering inclusive globalization
- Mitigating the impact of HIV/AIDS

Fostering democratic governance

- Fostering inclusive participation
- Strengthening responsive governing institutions
- Supporting national partners to implement democratic governance practices grounded in human rights, gender equality, and anti-corruption

Supporting crisis prevention and recovery

- Enhancing conflict and disaster risk-management capabilities
- Strengthening post-crisis governance functions
- Restoring the foundations for development

Managing energy and the environment for sustainable development

- Mainstreaming environment and energy
- Catalyzing environmental finance
- Promoting climate change adaptation
- Expanding access to environmental and energy services for the poor

Source: *UNDP Annual Report 2010: Delivering on Commitments*

Gender equality is another focus area within poverty reduction. Here, UNDP has maintained a rather ambiguous relationship with its affiliate organization UNIFEM, which—rather in the spirit of the competitive culture of the UN system—has steered an independent course with its own network of field representatives and projects.[10] By deferring to UNIFEM, gender considerations have not been adequately mainstreamed into UNDP's activities,[11] although country offices have implemented many individual women-oriented projects.

Aid management also falls into this cluster, but is an area where UNDP has lost ground to other organizations. In 1963, the World Bank began to organize and chair "consultative group meetings" for major recipient countries: initially Nigeria, Tunisia, Colombia, and Sudan. From 1966, the number of consultative group meetings increased, and by the end of the 1980s, 36 countries had held them.[12] In 1972, UNDP began to help least-developed countries (LDCs) to organize "round tables." The first of these were in Lesotho, Burkina Faso, Burundi, Benin, Central African Republic, and Djibouti, and the number grew after the 1981 LDC conference in Paris. The main difference from the consultative group meetings was that round tables were chaired by the governments concerned, but UNDP was active in helping with the preparations and raising awareness among prospective donors, for in practice these annual or biennial meetings were intended to mobilize resources. The number of UNDP round tables reached over 25 by the end of the 1980s, before declining. Some were taken over by the World Bank or a major donor country. Today, UNDP round tables are held for only a few countries in Asia and Africa.

As part of its work in aid management, UNDP was active in the past in publishing regular "development cooperation reports" for a large number of countries. These reports were a valuable and accurate source of information on all TA flows into a country, being based on the use of local questionnaires. The number of these reports has since declined, but UNDP continues to assist countries to set up aid data collection and management systems.

As in the World Bank, the poverty-reduction cluster is staffed largely by economists, and international trade is another of its focus areas. However, in this domain, expertise is spread very thinly as there have probably never been more than a dozen trade specialists on the UNDP staff at any one time. When the Integrated Framework for trade-related TA to LDCs was set up in 1997, UNDP was entrusted with managing the funds. But because it put few resources and staff into the task, this role was removed from it when the Integrated Framework was revamped and refinanced after 2006.

Democratic governance

Establishing governance as a fully fledged practice in UNDP in the later 1990s was a bold move, and was initially received with some reluctance by the developing countries on the Executive Board. They may have seen governance as a stalking horse for donor-country values and practices, but it was also bold because within countries it drew

UNDP into potentially sensitive policy areas, in contrast to the long-established reputation of the local UNDP offices as sources of friendly patronage. Since in most countries UNDP is a relatively small source of assistance, its advice may not command the same attention as better-heeled development partners. Yet promoting a specifically UN approach to governance challenges could be considered a comparative advantage.

In practice, some of the most visible aspects of the governance program have been in support of decentralization and local government institutions, assistance with electoral processes and parliamentary reform, and building capacity of human rights institutions. UNDP claims to be supporting an election somewhere in the world every two weeks and helping to strengthen one-third of all parliaments in its program countries.[13]

An outstandingly successful example of electoral support was in Indonesia in 1999. At a time when the interest from other donors was waning, the UNDP office played an instrumental role in preparing the country for its first free and fair elections following the Suharto dictatorship. It helped draft election laws, supported the independent electoral commission, and even encouraged the formation of political parties. The elections were the foundation for the subsequent democratic development of the country.[14] Less successful has been UNDP's involvement in national elections in countries such as Cambodia (in the 1990s) and, more recently, Afghanistan, where there was clearly no readiness for open democratic processes. In these cases, more sophisticated appraisals by the local UNDP offices might have obviated the expenditure of substantial amounts of resources.

UNDP has also sought to play a part in tackling corruption by working with anti-corruption agencies, and with civil society and media, in raising awareness and encouraging the implementation of the UN convention against corruption. Given the sensitivity of the subject, UNDP has also developed regional projects on anti-corruption, forming networks in Asia-Pacific and among Arab states to build solidarity and exchange experience.

Crisis prevention and recovery

The creation of this major practice in UNDP answers critics who claim that the organization has not adapted to evolving development challenges. Following the end of the Cold War, and the retreat from rival spheres of influence by the two ideological powers, the number of fragile and failing states has grown, and the complexity of reconstruction multiplied. The UN has had a very poor historical record of pre-visioning state frailty and collapse (in East and Central Africa, and elsewhere). Now it bears some of the responsibility for recovery, and here UNDP has anticipated that it has an important role to play.

This priority area is an odd mix of both human-made and natural crisis. The former is fundamentally a governance concern, with a conceptually awkward overlap with the democratic governance practice. The latter is more in the nature of humanitarian response, but with a nod to the environmental stresses that provoke natural disasters. What they have in common is the development of responses to crises of any kind that threaten lives and livelihoods. Latterly, the development problems associated with climate change have been added to the list of concerns.

UNDP has some special advantages in crisis response. It has boots on the ground in nearly every developing country, and is connected to a wide range of local government and civil interests. It can help coordinate assistance following a crisis—with UNDP resident representatives often acting as humanitarian coordinators—and in recovery phases, it can make the bridge from emergency to development aid. In 2009, UNDP provided conflict prevention and recovery services to no fewer than 87 countries, but in many cases it was helping in devising plans for future crisis response—including what the UN's curious terminology calls "natural disaster prevention." At the other end of the scale have been Iraq and Afghanistan—arguably the world's two most costly human-made crises. Here, UNDP has been entrusted with substantial resources by the international community (with spending in excess of $550 million in Afghanistan in 2009 alone) as a mark of confidence.

A 2006 evaluation of UNDP's activities in six conflict-affected countries was quite positive.[15] In difficult situations there are always many factors, remote from the theatres, which complicate responses, such as UN Security Council resolutions and adequacy of funding. Different UN and other actors also tend to crowd into a crisis opportunistically, and are initially resistant to coordination.[16] Generally, UNDP's role in coordination and resource mobilization was applauded. What is still needed is more depth in specific post-conflict skills in areas such as disarmament, demobilization, and reintegration; and administration of justice.

Energy and environment

UNDP always harbored some limited expertise in natural resources, including forestry and water. But it was after the Earth Summit in Rio de Janeiro in 1992 that it began to build its capacity. As was usual in UN phases of expansion, funding was the engine. UNDP fought hard, with support from developing countries, to ensure that the Global Environment Facility (GEF), incubated in the World Bank since 1991, would not remain solely a bank instrument. The GEF became a tripartite body in 1994, with UNDP and UNEP also sharing the resources. UNDP's special advantage at that time was its country network, which was much more extensive that those of its partners. But it also quickly developed its expertise in the three main areas targeted by the GEF: biodiversity, climate change, and international waters. In more recent years, the mandate of the GEF has expanded to include land degradation, the ozone layer, and persistent organic pollutants, and the partnership has expanded to ten organizations, including the International Fund for Agricultural Development (IFAD), FAO, and UNIDO from within the system (the four others being regional development banks).

The GEF was initially worth $150 million and its projects were, and have remained, the backbone of UNDP's work in the environmental domain. Several of the largest projects were trans-boundary and played to UNDP's strength in persuading contiguous countries to collaborate. (For many years, the largest project in Asia was UNDP's support to the Mekong committee of four riparian countries in Southeast Asia— Cambodia, Laos, Thailand, and Vietnam—during a period of delicate diplomacy.)

For some time, the best specialized expertise in UNDP has been in the environment and energy field, taking advantage of growing funds from the GEF, as well as other sources such as the Montreal Protocol (designed to roll back emissions of chlorofluorocarbons, which attack the Earth's ozone layer). Funding, in fact, has been the tail wagging the corporate dog. As a 2008 UNDP-wide evaluation determined, "UNDP corporate plans and strategies have had little influence on the selection of priorities and activities for the country programs. In practice, the availability of financial resources from GEF has had a far greater influence on the priority setting and choice of activities of country offices."[17] Influence on policy was generally weak, mainly because "most country offices lack the capacity to engage in high-level policy dialogue with the governments" (a weakness unfortunately not confined to this area). However, corporate strategy aside, UNDP could nevertheless point to some successful individual projects, as documented by the *Assessments of Development Results* which the evaluation office has undertaken in some 40 countries.

One of the general conclusions to be drawn from this brief overview of UNDP's effectiveness as a development organization is that, while the organization has succeeded in developing a critical mass of expertise in several strategic areas, the capacity has not been adequately absorbed or matched in many country offices. From close observation, these offices are staffed more with doers than thinkers and analysts. As UNDP tries to move upstream into more complex policy areas, this imbalance will only become more stark, especially when UNDP's country offices are compared with those of the World Bank, which has followed UNDP's lead in decentralizing its staff and building a strong country network of its own.

UN system coordinator

Another of the conclusions of the evaluation report cited above was that "the role of UNDP in environment and energy within the United Nations system is potentially central but not fully realized."[18] This conclusion could be generalized. At the country level, which accounts for the overwhelming proportion of the organization's activities, UNDP funds and implements its projects alongside those of other UN agencies, many working in similar fields. This parallelism is wasteful and, as this book has documented, it has steadily widened over time as more and more UN development system organizations have established a field presence. Thus the effectiveness of UNDP's role as coordinator can be judged by its ability to bring the UN system into a more harmonious alignment, in some cases taking an active implementation role itself, in others not.

Historically, the effectiveness of UNDP as "system coordinator" in the field was at its height at the time of its creation. The organization inherited from EPTA and the TAB an already large network of field staff who, in nearly every developing country, were the sole UN system representatives. They would have been familiar with most UN activities in their countries, and certainly all of those that UNDP was funding. Equally important, these representatives were in a position to relay to the rest of the development system the development needs of the countries in which they served.

As became clear from earlier chapters, however, UNDP's aspirations to become a development organization in its own right, as well as the frustrations that accompanied execution by UN agencies, led to a sharp diminution of its funding of the system, thus loosening the reins which UNDP held as a principal donor. It lost the loyalty of the UN agencies and organizations, which were, in a concomitant and wholly unrestrained process, steadily building their own networks of field representatives. In the capitals of most developing countries, it is now common to find more than ten UN offices. In some—even middle-income countries—there are 15 or more, even 20.[19]

As the number of UN country (and regional) representatives rose, so did the dangers of duplication and parallelism. General Assembly resolution 32/197 of 1977 sought to try to resolve the problems of proliferation by proposing the designation of a UN "resident coordinator" from among the local representatives. UNDP was not specifically designated as the lead agency, but in practice its own representatives were to become the UN resident coordinators in nearly every country. History played a part in this default decision, but UNDP also had the broadest (albeit least well-defined) development mandate.

Giving the field coordinator functions to UNDP was accepted, but not necessarily welcomed, by the rest of the system. It helped that, in the hierarchical rankings common to the UN system, the UNDP resident representatives were often the most senior among their peers. But there were two flaws in this expedient outcome. By proposing that an existing representative be designated as coordinator, thus combining two functions, the resolution provided an obvious advantage to UNDP as a favored beneficiary in any UN-wide initiatives. UNDP has taken full advantage of this privileged position, detracting from the objectivity which the coordinator posts should have exemplified.[20] To avoid this problem—which would have been the same whichever agency was designated as coordinator—the original resolution should have created wholly new posts for UN resident coordinators, at an elevated level.

The second and related flaw in this outcome was that UNDP in the field had project managers *par excellence*, but usually not development specialists. Ideally, a UN resident coordinator needed to be not only knowledgeable about the country, but also skilled in understanding and interpreting development needs, so as to be able to judge and apportion the roles of different agencies of the system. UN resident coordinators, in Jackson's original words, needed to be the "brains" of the system at the country level. With few exceptions, this was not—and still is not—the profile of the UNDP resident representatives.

Periodically, different arrangements for the administration of the UN coordinators have been discussed in New York, but the UNDP default option has always prevailed. Two further attempts have been made to create greater coherence at country level. The first—discussed in Chapter 2—was the creation of unified offices in the republics of the former Soviet Union in 1992. These offices began as an awkward joint venture between the field-oriented UNDP and the centrist UN secretariat. But the concept was sound in principle: having a single coordinator representing the whole UN development system meant that no agency had an inside track, and a country's needs could be addressed holistically. These offices would have been even more effective had knowledgeable outsiders been appointed to head them. In practice, rival UN agencies perceived them as giving UNDP an unfair advantage, and they were undermined by lobbying in New York.

Full unification has not been attempted since. However, UNDP and the UNDG in New York, comprising most of the development system organizations, have encouraged the formation of "country teams" of local UN representatives, chaired by the UN resident coordinator. In these teams, UNDP is also represented by the deputy UN resident representative. In order to make a clearer separation between its development and coordination interests, UNDP has named a growing number of "country directors" to head up its program work, allowing the resident coordinator to concentrate more exclusively on system functions. UNDP has also actively sought to widen the catchment for resident coordinator candidates, bringing in a growing number from other agencies and organizations, and from outside the UN. The coordinators are still administered by UNDP, but their identity with the organization has been diluted. All have to undergo a selection process that consists of a number of management and communications tests over three days, in which success is not guaranteed. The one critical element that is absent from this screening process, however, is any test of development knowledge and skills. Successful candidates still, therefore, emerge from the traditional (non-substantive) UNDP mold.

The 2006 reform program *Delivering as One*[21] proposed "unified United Nations country teams – with one leader, one programme, one budgetary framework and, where appropriate, one office." There were to be five pilot One UN countries initially, since grown to eight,[22] with more showing interest. These proposals were fully embraced by UNDP, and in the eight countries some progress has been made in tightening the cohesion of the country teams. Again, funding holds the key to success. These and other countries now benefit from multi-donor trust funds, which are intended to be apportioned among the agencies on the basis of development need, as defined by a unified program framework. In practice, all resident agencies—and non-resident agencies adept at lobbying—expect to receive shares. In these countries, there are now more joint (multi-agency) programs, but they resemble packages of parallel projects and can themselves entail complex problems of sequencing and coordination. Delivering as one at the country level tests the capacities of the system to work more harmoniously in parallel, but may involve more, not less, time and resources. Above all, what are lacking are those respected UN development specialists who can evaluate development needs for their countries comprehensively, and apportion and adjudicate the contributions of different parts of the UN system, on an objective—rather than mainly expedient—basis.

Because of its management of the UN resident coordinator network, UNDP takes responsibility for system coordination at the global level through the UNDG, which includes most of the agencies and organizations involved in development operations. UNDP's administrator—who is the third most senior UN official after the Secretary-General and Deputy Secretary-General—has a second role as UNDG chair (see Chapter 2).

The first administrator to chair the UNDG was Gustave Speth in 1997. At that time, the membership was quite limited, but since then it has expanded to include most of the UN entities involved in TA. Typically for the UN, however, there was no deliberate process of determining eligibility, resulting in anomalies. Among standards organizations, the International Telecommunication Union (ITU) is included, but the Universal Postal Union (UPU) and the International Maritime Organization (IMO) are not; in the trade field, UNCTAD is included, but the more operational ITC (designated as the principal trade promotion body of the UN) is not. Also included are other UN offices within the New York secretariat, with no responsibilities for field operations. The UNDG—and its secretariat, the UN Development Operations Coordination Office (UNDOCO)—is nevertheless an effective mechanism for maintaining a dialogue within the UN development system, and was instrumental in implementing the recent One UN initiative.

Whatever the commitment of UNDP, however, UN system coordination will remain complex and burdensome as long as most parts of the system have their own independent governance mechanisms. The Economic and Social Council, established by the UN Charter, was intended to exercise system oversight, but the pusillanimous language of chapter X ("it may co-ordinate the activities of the specialized agencies through consultation etc [...]"[23]) vested it with a weak mandate. Reform (read: strengthening) of ECOSOC has been an exhortation in almost every UN reform process. UNDP and UNFPA share the same executive board[24] and there are now joint sessions every year with UNICEF and WFP. However, these are forums for discussion of common concerns, rather mechanisms of integration.

Efficiency

If effectiveness is equated with impacts external to the organization, this section looks more closely at the internal metrics and the successive organizational reform processes.

Among other UN entities, UNDP was an innovator in terms of internal reform. The first serious attempts were undertaken in the 1980s by Bill Draper, an Administrator with strong private-sector instincts. While UNDP may have paid a heavy price within the UN for his strong desire to downplay family loyalty, he brought to the organization some valuable corporate practices. Two in particular were significant for UNDP's efficiency, both intended to enrich human resources. One was a more aggressive and direct approach to the recruitment of new staff, involving visits to some of the best universities in Europe and North America to advertise careers in development. Country offices were also mobilized to hunt heads amongst counterparts in government and civil society, but also the private sector. There was also a strong new emphasis on training. Management experts were brought in, and everyone in the middle and upper ranks in headquarters underwent courses on team-playing and communications. Apart from the skills imparted, this commitment to staff was a fillip to morale.

Comprehensive reforms followed with the next two administrations. In 1996, under Gustave Speth, came UNDP 2001, which (despite its name) was mostly completed in 1999, when a new Administrator took over. The first years of the Malloch Brown tenure saw a further phase of change management, described in Chapter 3. Each process of reform was preceded by intensive introspection about the kind of organization which UNDP wanted to be and its place in the development cooperation firmament. What made UNDP so amenable to change was the constant challenge of trying to redefine itself, and the bifurcated nature of its functions, which this chapter has described.

There have been several comparative analyses of multilateral organizations in recent years. In 2005, the UK Department for International Development (DFID) published the results of its Multilateral Effectiveness Framework, which made an assessment of the organizational effectiveness of 23 multilateral bodies, mostly in the UN system during 2003–04.[25] Their scorecard was based on internal performance, country-level results, and partnership. Organizations were also classified by the scale of their reform, with UNDP in the "big bang" category. DFID was clearly impressed with the reform process because it ranked UNDP first on internal performance (with 96 percent), well ahead of other UN agencies and the World Bank (86 percent). UNDP was also top-ranked for the other two categories.

However, in 2008, another more extensive survey of multilateral and bilateral agencies, using different criteria of efficiency, gave a very different picture.[26] The survey examined "best practices" in aid administration in a total of 40 organizations, including several from the UN system. When judged by "transparency" (of aid data as well as internal administrative details), UNDP was ranked 12th, above the other UN organizations, but below the World Bank (1st) and most of the regional development banks. A much more ominous finding was on "overhead costs," where UNDP was ranked 34th out of 35 (only WFP was worse). The survey determined that the ratio of the administrative budget of UNDP to actual development assistance was 129 percent, and that salary costs on their own were 100 percent, i.e. equal to the value of all TA. These figures were very substantially higher than any other bilateral organization or development bank. The amount of assistance per permanent employee was calculated as $0.19, far below the majority of agencies.

The study cited points to the difficulty of obtaining accurate data and the hazards of comparison. The costs of administering TA are bound to be higher than lending by banks. The World Bank's administrative costs are estimated at only 7 percent (although it is also a source of grant TA larger than UNDP's). But comparisons with bilateral donors are also unfavorable. The fact that Norway's bilateral disbursement per employee is more than 50 times that of UNDP, says the study, makes it difficult "to believe that this degree of variation is due to differences in effectiveness between UNDP and Norway."[27] This contrast is so stark between UNDP and its largest core donor that there have to be other explanations for the differences.

The most obvious one is that UNDP is not just a development agency, but an extensive network of offices with responsibilities that range outside its own project management needs, including services to other agencies. Bilateral agencies, on the other hand, can enlist the services of diplomatic missions and embassies for part of their aid management needs and these costs are not factored into the totals. Also, the data are probably based on core resources, whereas UNDP is a major conduit of funds from non-core[28] sources, which would help to improve the ratios. But the figures are still striking in absolute and comparative terms, and the reality is that UNDP has a lot of expensive administrative infrastructure. To understand this better, it is only necessary to examine the profile of a typical UNDP country office.

UNDP offices (like those of other UN organizations) are accorded diplomatic status, and they have some of the characteristics of embassies, at least in terms of hierarchy. The head of the office (resident representative or country director) has two deputies, one for program matters, the other for administration. These are usually international staff. The deputies, in their turn, manage one (usually more) assistant resident representatives, who manage teams of national officers. There are therefore four layers of responsibility, with the top three delegating downwards. The head of the office, if a UNDP resident representative, is concurrently the UN resident coordinator, and in these functions will have a separate staff team. In addition to these core staff, there may be other shorter-term staff, including junior professional officers funded separately by donors,[29] and consultants. Each office will have its own finance unit (there is very little pooling among UN agencies, and limited outsourcing) and a logistics team comprising several drivers, messengers, and filing clerks.[30]

During Malloch Brown's tenure, UNDP made a serious attempt to rationalize its field staff through "reprofiling," but it is not clear how successful it was in flattening the office hierarchies and reducing the amount of time staff spend just managing other people. In any case, whatever economies made in slimming the country offices would have been outweighed by the decision to create a fully fledged regional structure in UNDP (see Chapter 3).

What is also telling about this analysis, however, is the generally poor performance of the UN agencies in general. The conclusions to be drawn are that the continued fragmentation of the development system at country level and the co-existence of many small UN offices each with their separate staffs, administrations, and offices is highly cost-ineffective. When the UNDP reprofiling exercise was in progress, country offices complained about the etiolation of their professional staff, leaving them with limited capacity in several areas. But taken as a whole, the UN family of agencies, present in almost every developing country, represents an impressive professional cohort with a wide range of specializations and experience. Reprofiling was an opportunity to establish much closer connections with the staff in other agencies. But despite moves toward common programming, cross-agency teamwork is still the exception.

In order to assist with agency consolidation, the UN has pursued the creation of single "UN houses" containing all the agencies and organizations within each country. Starting with South Africa in 1996, the number has grown to 55 in 2010, although in a few cases one or more humanitarian agencies are not included (e.g. WFP) because of their more substantial vehicle and logistics needs. The UN house concept is far from fully implemented, but it is a valuable step toward further consolidation of the system and greatly facilitates the possibility of pooling facilities, which would result in greater cost-effectiveness.

Conclusion

In early 2010, the Multilateral Organization Performance Assessment Network (MOPAN) of 16 donor countries[31] published its latest assessment of UNDP. MOPAN examines organizational effectiveness in terms of strategic, operational, relationship, and knowledge management, using a total of 18 indicators. On 14 of these indictors, UNDP's performance was "adequate," while it was "strong" in two and "weak" in two others. The survey (conducted in 2009 and based on a questionnaire of UNDP's partners in nine countries) summarized its findings as follows:

> The UNDP continues to be recognized for the role that it plays in development aid architecture at the country level: its role in coordinating government and other UN agencies is cited by several respondents as its greatest organizational strength [...] this perception is also reflected in the importance given to the UNDP's decentralized decision making and its contributions to policy dialogues. Responses confirm several factors that have posed challenges to the UNDP over the years: the perceived breadth of its mandate, on the one hand, and perceptions of a high level of bureaucracy in the organization.[32]

MOPAN conflated UNDP's two roles in its analysis. But an assessment of UNDP's performance cannot ignore its split organizational personality. As a development agency, very gradually narrowing its domains of interest, it has sought to diminish the collisions with other parts of the system, with some success. But the honing at HQ has not been fully reflected at the field level, which is where the huge majority of staff are to be found. In countries, MOPAN still finds the "breadth of mandate" in UNDP to be a challenge. And to the extent that there has been more focus at country level, UNDP lacks the depth of expertise of the World Bank and other development agencies. While it may aspire to move upstream as a policy interlocutor, its credentials fall short. MOPAN found its contribution to policy dialogue to be "focused more on its role as coordinator and less on making substantive contributions of its own."[33]

The question arises, therefore: can UNDP ever be a superior performer as an agency of development specializations while it is spread so thinly in staff and resources? The World Bank has almost the same geographic universality, but with much stronger staff and financial resources. Other multilateral and bilateral agencies concentrate more intensively on fewer countries.

As a system coordinator, UNDP's performance is subject to factors that, in many cases, are beyond its immediate control. The attempts of successive reforms to put UNDP back into the center are frustrated by the jealously guarded independence of all parts of the UN development system, resulting in unsatisfactory and ambiguous outcomes. UNDP has been saddled with managing ever more elaborate mechanisms of coordination, when integration would be a superior and more cost-effective goal. But UNDP's dual role also poses difficulties. UNDP openly competes with its fellow agencies for the same sources of patronage. And its internal culture is so imbued with resource mobilization concerns that there is a reluctance about sharing resources earmarked as multi-agency.

The general conclusion of this chapter is that UNDP's relevance and effectiveness cannot be best served while it continues to pursue its two roles. But rather than summarily abandoning its role as a development organization, it can begin to shift toward areas of broad UN concern, in which it can play a role of leading and convening other UN entities. A prime example stems from the role of "campaign manager and score-keeper" of the MDGs, to which UNDP elected itself in 2001. Although the UN system was slow in recognizing the MDGs as its common agenda, nearly every agency has a mandate that touches on one or more of the goals (see Box 3.1) and now considers their achievement to be a priority. The MDGs are both universal and country-specific, since they aim at making proportionate improvements over country-determined baselines. As part of the score-keeping role, UNDP country offices already prepare periodic reports on MDG achievement, and UN resident coordinators are well-placed to mobilize the different parts of the UN system in support. It is also appropriate that the UN's "global development network" should play the role of campaign manager in aggregating progress toward MDG achievement, drawing on the statistical expertise of UN DESA, but using the advocacy skills that it applies to the HDRs. This role would be further enhanced if donors were to put more MDG-related funds through UNDP, as called for by the 2006 reform. The current Administrator has made the MDGs a central focus. Taking the torch at the front of the column would be a good example of how UNDP could again be perceived as a leader of the system.

5   The future of the UN development system

- Defining the "system"
- Problems with the system
- Global perceptions
- The long history of reform
- Why reform fails
- Conclusion: revisiting the past

Previous chapters have traced the evolution of UNDP and analyzed its effectiveness and performance within the larger UN development system. Having moved off its original base as the TA fund of the system, UNDP has pursued a dual role. As a development organization, it competes with other parts of the UN system for funds and attention, but more especially with the World Bank, which has become a substantial presence in developing countries, in terms of resources and influence. UNDP has also retained a coordination role, by dint of history and because of its broad mandate. But the two roles do not sit easily. The tension is not as evident within UNDP as it is from elsewhere in the system, where agencies would like to see a more evident firewall between the two roles.

This final chapter gives fuller attention to the UN development system. As the institutional context for UNDP, the system is defined and analyzed and its shortcomings are outlined in terms of its continuing relevance and effectiveness. Because it has had an impact on UNDP's role, this chapter also reviews the long saga of attempted reforms of the system, and the reasons for their failure. The final sections conclude that successive reform proposals of the system have been broadly consistent, based on which it sketches a future structure that would draw UNDP and the development system back to a configuration that resembles its starting point in the 1950s.

Defining the "system"

As it has been in the past, and continues to be in the present, the future of UNDP is bound up with the future of the UN development system. But what kind of a system has it become?

The system may be defined as all those parts of the UN—whether organization, program, fund, or specialized agency—that undertake activities on behalf of developing and transition-economy countries with longer-term human, social, and economic objectives.[1] The system considered here numbers over 30 different UN entities, the exact number depending on whether it includes the WFP (which is mainly, but not exclusively, a humanitarian agency), and organizations such as UNOPS, which is a procurement and project management agency serving both UN and non-UN clients.

Outside this definition of the system, but ancillary to it, are five training and research organizations (including the UN University based in Tokyo, but with several of its own specialized institutes), and eight "functional commissions" under ECOSOC. The World Bank is in a formal sense part of the system, but it operates largely independently (Figure 5.1).

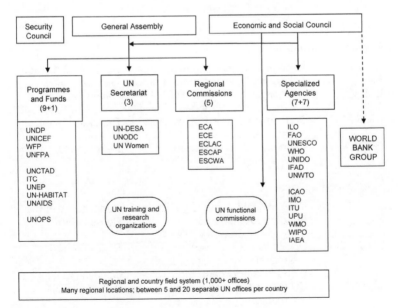

Figure 5.1 UN development system—existing structure

Box 5.1 The UN alphabet soup

Funds and programs		Seat (founding year)
UNDP	UN Development Programme	New York (1965)
UNICEF	UN Children's Fund	New York (1946)
WFP	World Food Programme	Rome (1963)
UNFPA	UN Population Fund	New York (1969)
UNCTAD	UN Conference on Trade and Development	Geneva (1964)
ITC	International Trade Centre	Geneva (1964)
UNEP	UN Environment Programme	Nairobi (1972)
UN-HABITAT	Human Settlements	Nairobi (1978)
UNAIDS	UN Joint Programme on HIV and AIDS	Geneva (1996)

UN Secretariat

UN DESA	UN Department of Economic and Social Affairs	New York (1945)
UNODC	UN Office of Drugs and Crime	Vienna (1997)*
UNOPS	UN Office of Project Services	Copenhagen (1973)
UN Women	UN Entity for Gender Equality and the Empowerment of Women	New York (2010)

Regional commissions

ECA	Economic Commission for Africa	Addis Ababa (1958)
ECE	Economic Commission for Europe	Geneva (1947)
ECLAC	Economic Commission for Latin America and Caribbean	Santiago (1948)
ESCAP	Economic Commission for Asia and Pacific	Bangkok (1949)
ESCWA	Economic Commission for West Asia	Beirut (1973)

Specialized agencies

ILO	International Labour Organization	Geneva (1919)
FAO	Food and Agriculture Organization of the UN	Rome (1945)
UNESCO	UN Educational, Scientific and Cultural Organization	Paris (1945)
WHO	World Health Organization	Geneva (1948)*
UNIDO	UN Industrial Development Organization	Vienna (1985)#

Funds and programs		Seat (founding year)
IFAD	International Fund for Agricultural Development	Rome (1977)
UNWTO	UN World Tourism Organization	Madrid (2003)*#
ICAO	International Civil Aviation Organization	Montreal (1945)
IMO	International Maritime Organization	London (1958)
WMO	World Meteorological Organization	Geneva (1951)*
WIPO	World Intellectual Property Organization	Geneva (1970)*
IAEA	International Atomic Energy Agency	Vienna (1957)

Training and research institutions

UNITAR	UN Institute for Training and Research	
UNICRI	UN Interregional Crime and Justice Research Institute	
UNIDIR	UN Institute for Disarmament Research	
UNRISD	UN Research Institute for Social Development	
UNU	UN University	

Functional commissions

	Sustainable development
	Narcotic drugs
	Crime prevention
	Science and technology
	Status of women
	Population and development
	Social development
	Statistics

Notes:
* Different name/status prior to UN.
# Date of joining UN as specialized agency.

The UN development system is therefore not easy to define, and to defenders of the *status quo* the "system" is something of a straw man. It is not really a system at all, but a very loose family of institutions linked mainly by an emblem, an ill-defined sense of idealism, and a common set of employment conditions. The system began to come together in 1945, encompassing the organizations from the nineteenth and early twentieth centuries—the ITU created in 1865, the Universal Postal Union (UPU) in 1874, and the ILO in 1919[2]—as well as those created in the immediate postwar period, including UNESCO and FAO (1945). UNICEF (1946) and WHO (1948) were founded on pre-existing organizations. New organizations were created later: UNCTAD and the ITC in 1964, UNDP in 1966, then UNFPA (1969), UNEP (1972), IFAD (1977), and the UN Human Settlements Programme (UN-HABITAT) (1978). The most recent adherents to the system are the Joint UN Programme on HIV/AIDS (UNAIDS, 1996), an offshoot of WHO, and the World Tourism Organization (UNWTO) originally founded in 1934 under a different name, which became part of the UN in 2003. In 2010, the newest member of the family, UN Women, was inaugurated. The UN development system has thus been over 150 years in formation—so far.

Even though related in some manner to long-term development, there are—as well as a varied vintages—also wide differences of function within the system. ITU and UPU were examples from the nineteenth century of "public international unions,"[3] in this case serving to facilitate global communications through functional coordination. Other UN agencies of a similar kind have emerged for shipping (IMO) and civil aviation (ICAO). Thus half (seven) of today's 14 UN specialized agencies are concerned primarily with international standards and norms. Some of the other specialized agencies have normative functions (like WHO), but are also operational. IFAD is a lending organization. UNCTAD and the five regional commissions are inter-governmental policy forums, but also with operational characteristics. UNCTAD, like the UN DESA, is also engaged in research and information. UNDP and ITC are almost purely operational, but UNDP also undertakes original research. The pattern of functions, together with the sizes of the UN system entities (staff and expenditure), is shown in Table 5.1.

Problems with the system

If the sheer heterogeneity of the "system" can be an argument for abandoning any pretence of calling it one, globally there is a huge moral commitment to a universal organization, both for keeping the peace and for helping the cause of human development. With so much in place—organizationally and financially—there is a case for examining

Table 5.1 UN development system: functions and size

Agency/ organization	Technical services					Staff*	Annual expenditure ($m 2008 or latest year)
	Technical standards and norms	Intergovern- mental cooperation and policy	Advocacy, conventions	Research data, information	Technical assistance		
UN SECRETARIAT							
DESA		√		√	√	509	69
UNODC		√	√	√	√	467	231
FUNDS AND PROGRAMS							
UNDP			√	√	√	5,402	4,270
UNICEF	√		√	√	√	6,430	2,808
WFP	√	√	√		√	9,139	3,536
UNFPA			√	√	√	1,719	436
UNCTAD		√	√	√	√	500	35
ITC					√	290	49
UNEP	√	√	√	√	√	994	131
UN-HABITAT		√	√	√	√	341	125
UNAIDS			√	√	√	400	142

(continued on next page)

Table 5.1 (continued)

Agency/ organization	Technical services					Staff*	Annual expenditure ($m 2008 or latest year)
	Technical standards and norms	Intergovern-mental cooperation and policy	Advocacy, conventions	Research data, information	Technical assistance		
REGIONAL COMMISSIONS							
ECA		√√		√	√	644	59
ECE		√√		√	√	171	
ECLAC		√√		√	√	460	
ESCAP		√√		√	√	522	
ESCWA		√√		√	√	330	
SPECIALIZED AGENCIES							
ILO	√√	√		√√	√	2,500	424
FAO	√	√	√	√	√√	3,600	691
UNESCO	√	√	√	√	√√	2,160	347
WHO	√√	√√	√√	√	√√	8,000	1,691
UNIDO	√	√	√	√	√√	650	231
IFAD				√	√√	436	450

Table 5.1 (continued)

| Agency/ organization | Technical services | | | | | Staff* | Annual expenditure ($m 2008 or latest year) |
	Technical standards and norms	Intergovern-mental cooperation and policy	Advocacy, conventions	Research data, information	Technical assistance		
UNWTO		√|		√		90	379
ICAO	√|	√	√		√	700	
IMO	√|	√	√		√	300	
ITU	√|	√	√		√	822	
UPU	√|	√	√		√	230	
WMO	√|	√	√		√	300	
WIPO	√|	√	√		√	939	
IAEA	√|	√	√		√	2,200	
TOTALS						51,245	16,104**

Sources: www.un.org/esa/cordination/dcpb_stat.htm; FUNDS project
Notes:
√| = primary function
* excluding short-term and project staff
** includes humanitarian assistance (mainly WFP and UNICEF) of approximately $2.5 billion

why the UN does not work better in the development field, what has been done to try to improve it, and what could be a vision for the future.

This section adumbrates the problems, which can be succinctly summed up as the diminishing capacity of the UN development system to address the global challenges for which it originally came together. As a former deputy Secretary-General puts it, "the honest judgment on accumulated decades of effort is that while different bits of the UN system have been able to move ahead and improve performance, as a whole, the gap between capacity and demand is increasing. The world wants more of the UN and the organization is only able to deliver less."[4] As for UNDP (Chapter 4), the weaknesses can be headlined under relevance and effectiveness.

Relevance

In contrast to the 1950s, when the development system was coming together, today there are many alternatives to the UN, in each of its different functions. In global standard-setting, some UN organizations are still recognized as pre-eminent, such as WHO in the health field. But standards are not an inter-governmental preserve. For example, one of the best known and most effective global standard-setting organizations is the nongovernmrntal ISO, which has, according to a recent book, "taken on some of the tasks that have proven too difficult for the UN."[5] These include environmental standards, labor rights, and corporate responsibility, for which different parts of the system also claim responsibility. In the communications field, one of the internet governance mechanisms is another NGO, the Internet Corporation for Assigned Names and Numbers (ICANN), which many stakeholders did not want to come under the jurisdiction of ITU.

In the information domain, the UN still prevails in certain areas. One of the best-known is demography, where the population division of UN DESA is still the global reference. The UN system is also an authoritative source for data and information in areas such as food, health, HIV/AIDS, drug control, and urbanization. In areas such as trade, industry, tourism, and environment, however, there are author-itative non-UN alternatives. Development research is even more com-petitive. Apart from the World Bank and the regional development banks, there are many sources of high-quality research in universities and think tanks around the world.

Inter-governmental cooperation and policy-making is more central to the UN's potential role in global governance. But in economics, finance, and trade, the UN is being marginalized. In the aftermath of both the Asian financial crisis of 1996–97 and the global financial crisis of 2008–09, the UN was scarcely visible. In the latter case, the new G20 group of developed and developing countries came together to forge policy. As a trade forum, UNCTAD has been steadily eclipsed by the WTO, which is by choice formally outside the UN. WTO's role has grown *pari passu* with an expansion in membership, which now includes the large majority of developed and developing countries. At the regional level, the UN's regional commissions were specifically established as cooperative forums. However, partly due to their success in helping to foster new regional and sub-regional arrangements, there are now many alternative inter-governmental bodies in all the regions.

Advocacy has been a strong UN feature in development areas such as environmental management, gender equality, drug control, human trafficking, and anti-corruption measures. There are also many non-UN and nongovernmrntal advocates in these areas, but the system can give a UN imprimatur to advocacy campaigns and draw up global conventions. The problem is the "compliance gap."[6] Universal ratification of UN conventions is the exception and, beyond the moral, the UN has no financial or other leverage to enforce compliance, unlike the World Bank and IMF.

Finally, in the domain of TA, the UN system role has become increasingly crowded out by many alternative sources. As an example, UNDP once called itself the largest source of grant-based multilateral TA, but was overtaken by the World Bank many years ago.[7] Other development banks have also grown in importance, and the largest source of all is the European Commission. These and the bilateral donors—to which must be added major private sources such as the Gates and Soros Foundations—provide high-quality services and expertise which are often more relevant to developing country needs. Perhaps equally significant are the development services that developing countries choose and purchase for themselves from private sources.

A measure of relevance is the relative importance of UN in aid funding. The share of the UN in total aid from the OECD/DAC countries was almost 10 percent in 2000. This is an increase compared with previous years, but the growth was largely attributable to humanitarian assistance. The proportion fell back to barely 5 percent in 2009, according to OECD/DAC data.[8] Within total multilateral assistance, the UN share has declined from about a quarter to less than one-fifth (19 percent for the period 2004–08). Aid from the European Commission—classified as multilateral here—has increased commensurately (Figure 5.2).

The data are for "core" funding. In fact, the UN development system has continued to grow because of large increases in "non-core" funding from the same major donors of the system, supplemented more recently by funding from the European Commission. In 1993, non-core funding to the UN development system was 30 percent of the total; the figure is now 70 percent. The OECD classifies this funding as bilateral, since it is provided—*through* rather than *to* the UN—for specific purposes or countries. When total funding is considered, the system cannot be said to have lost ground so much as transformed itself into a larger conduit of bilateral assistance. But the more directed the funding, the more it distorts the multilateral nature of the UN.

Relevance is also about supply meeting demand. The funding story shows that the UN development system has remained dominated by a limited number of rich countries, and is consequently as much supply-driven as demand-driven. Taking core and non-core resources together, in 2008 the OECD/DAC countries still contributed 57 percent of the total resources to UN development (excluding humanitarian assistance); 62 percent if the EC is included as a non-core contributor. Of course, there is a greater diversity of sources compared with the dominant era of the United States in the 1950s and 1960s. However, the continuing preponderant weight of the rich countries in UN development, and the growth in steered non-core resources, has inevitably introduced distortions.

As this book makes clear, the pre-financing of TA by donors leads to a bias of aid in favor of rich-country agendas,[9] and this applies to the

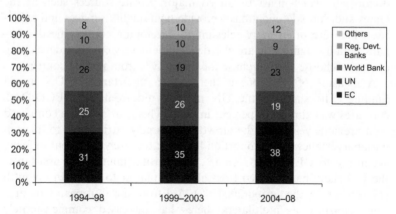

Figure 5.2 UN share of multilateral aid, 1994–2008

multilateral system as well as the bilateral. Within every UN organization and agency, secretariats instinctively "follow the money." Wherever it has become clear that donors are willing to fund a particular initiative or program, a suitable proposal is sure to follow. In UNDP, the administrator Paul Hoffman started a population program in the 1960s, encouraged by the interest of the United States and other donors. By 1969, there was a fully fledged agency (UNFPA). In more recent years, the emergence of the democratic governance, conflict prevention, and ICT for development priorities in UNDP was in large part motivated initially by funding prospects. In the latter case, the practice closed after a few years, not for lack of interest from developing countries but because it became clear that funds would not be forthcoming on a significant scale. In UNDP and other agencies, the creation of programs on women in development, environmental management, and other major areas has been encouraged and sustained by donor funding interest.

There is little doubt that all these donor-driven initiatives have provided benefits to developing countries. However, donor influence has led to distortions in the UN development system: structural distortions because the domains more popular with donors have led to a proliferation of programs; and operational distortions because donor-favored programs draw resources away from other areas, and because donors like to exert their own policy influence (one of the more extreme examples being the complete withdrawal of US funds from UNFPA from 2002 to 2009 over abortion issues, discussed in Chapter 1). Specifically, the UN system has not been adequately responsive in many policy areas that are of critical interest to developing countries, but not to donors. The UN Centre on Transnational Corporations was established in 1974 to help developing countries negotiate advantageous agreements with multinational corporations, but closed later under duress.[10] At different times, the UN has also been warned off— or not been given support in—areas such as South–South cooperation; intellectual property as a development (as opposed to a purely protectionist) issue; debt forgiveness; aid conditionality; trade protectionism by developed countries; commodity price stabilization; and other global economic issues on which policy has been dominated by the donor-controlled Bretton Wood institutions. As a sympathetic study of the UN system put it recently:

> The economic arena is where the UN has appeared more marginal [...] has had less visibility, has almost always had less clout, and accordingly has had less impact and implementation. This was not

because of lack of ideas [...] but rather because many of the ideas
ran counter to current orthodoxies and the economic interests of
the richer and more powerful countries.[11]

A more positive trend in the funding of the system, however, por-
tends a more responsive UN system in the future and is earmarked
here for later consideration. It is manifested by the slowly rising proportion of what the UN calls "local resource contributions," which are
made to the UN by developing countries themselves, usually for the
purchase of services from UNDP, but also from some other agencies
(mainly UNICEF, WFP, UNODC, FAO, UNESCO, and ICAO). By
2008, this source represented about 10 percent of total non-core contributions, and demonstrates the value that beneficiary countries place
on some parts of the UN system. The major contributors in 2008 were
mainly middle-income countries: in order of contribution size they
were Brazil, Panama, Argentina, Colombia, Peru, Egypt, Iraq, Honduras,
Afghanistan, and China.

Effectiveness

The relative decline in the UN's position as a superior provider of
multilateral assistance would have occurred as a natural result of many
emerging alternative sources of development cooperation. However,
there is little doubt that a loss of "competitiveness" has been hastened
by several negative trends that are internal to the system.

One has been remarked on frequently already, and that is a lack of
coherence. The architecture of the system was flawed from the outset,
with responsibilities shared among many power centers: the UN
secretariat, invariably headed by a peacemaker-in-chief, presiding over
a group of funds and programs, on one side; and on the other, a collection of 14 independently governed specialized agencies—located in
eight different cities of Europe and North America—for whose heads
"coordination" has always been anathema. A recent writer has hesitated
between calling it "feudal system or dysfunctional family."[12]

A major cause of UN atomization is also related to funding patterns.
Rich-country donors have been generous with the UN system, but the
fact that they like to patronize many of its individual parts in parallel
leads to furious competition among agencies and organizations for a
portion of the bounty. There is probably no other factor that more
effectively drives the system apart, and until more pooling is achieved
through multi-donor, multi-agency, multi-country funding mechanisms,
disunity will prevail.

The UN system also needs a trusted center to receive and responsibly allocate pooled funds. There is none, however, and consequently the system has whirled on several axes, continually proliferating. Agreement by all the UN heads to meet twice a year with the Secretary-General in the chair is little more than symbolic, despite recent attempts to formalize more inter-agency arrangements. At the country level, there are at least UN teams which meet quite frequently. These teams help to close up the parallel lines, but do not achieve real convergence. At the regional level, where the concern about coherence is very new, there is no convergence at all.

This degree of organizational discombobulation might not seem to matter. Having different parts of the system competing rather than cooperating can be a spur to improvement. But it does matter, because the world still needs a United Nations to provide neutral, value-based and people-friendly UN approaches to many global challenges and, as currently structured and operated, the system dissembles and dissimulates rather than effectively discharging these functions. The recent attempts by the UN to respond to global crises in finance, food security and global warming have exemplified the problems of harnessing ideas and action in a timely manner.[13] Above all, without a strategic center the UN system lacks an agenda. Starting in the 1960s, the UN development decades were intended as frameworks and objectives for UN activities. But no clearly articulated action plans resulted. The elaborately expounded human development concept emanated from UNDP in the 1990s, but was never translated into an operational framework. Even when the clearest global development agenda of all was signed up to by the largest gathering of heads of state in history—the Millennium Declaration of September 2000—the system was slow to react. It was several years before all the organizations and agencies recognized the Millennium Development Goals as a focus of their operations.

Nor has the system moved with the times. When new agencies were being created in the 1940s, the world looked very different. Governments were more powerful and encompassing. "Development" was assumed to progress within economic and social sectors, for each of which there was a ministry, and the UN system largely mirrored these national government structures (FAO for agriculture, UNIDO for industry, WHO for health, and so on). Although new UN entities have emerged in areas such as population, environment, and urbanization (just as there have been new ministries), the UN's operations still mostly respond to counterparts in traditional ministries. Today, when there is a better understanding of the dynamics of the development process, and of the major role played in almost every country by private enterprise, the UN system has not adequately adjusted to the changing role of the state as facilitator rather than doer, and has not developed a closer understanding of the private sector.[14] One of the manifestations of the UN's slowness to adapt has been the successful emergence of major public–private partnership organizations, such as the World Economic Forum and the Clinton Global Initiative. These organizations will not supplant the UN, but they provide valuable examples of how the system could more effectively embrace the concept of partnerships.

There are also many specific technical areas in which the UN has yet to develop the kind of responses which today's developing countries need, a small sample of which would include: modern organizational and management practices, effective media and communications, and innovative energy systems. The system is also steeped in old-fashioned methods of "delivering" services, rather than catalyzing processes. Traditional training methods are a good example. There are still thousands of face-to-face meetings and expert missions, where more online or other interactive learning processes would be more effective, as well as less costly. There is also a poor general understanding of how capacity, in its various dimensions, can be developed.

Within itself, the UN family also lacks effective operational systems which could help to enhance coherence. The common staff system and the pension scheme—perhaps the only features which justify calling the UN a system—have important practical value, since they facilitate the transfer of personnel and, in principle, render conditions of service more uniform. However, the common system is open to widespread interpretation and there are significant variations in conditions and remuneration in the different field-based services of the UN. Unfortunately, salary levels have been kept well below those of other multilateral organizations by the General Assembly and they have not been competitive for many years. Partly in consequence, the quality of staff working across the whole system is extremely varied, and poor at worst. Staff quality is also compromised by the rigid application of national quotas in some parts of the UN, and casual non-competitive hiring practices.

One of the greatest single lacuna is the inadequacy of the UN system to manage knowledge. Forty years ago, Robert Jackson's *Capacity Study* called for a unified information system (see Chapter 1), but even long after the advent of electronic communications, no means exists for the extraordinary amount of knowledge and experience across the UN system to be captured and shared. UNDP has pioneered its own internal knowledge networks, but these are not yet accessible by other agencies, except on a very limited basis.

Internal exchange is also hampered by the absence of a common enterprise resource planning (ERP) system, for managing human resources, salary payments, contracting, and other practical tasks. The UN has one, and some of its own organizations and many of the UN agencies have their own. However, again because there was no strategic center to ordain a uniform process, each entity went its own way and made its own choices of software. Most notoriously, UNDP—for entirely parochial reasons—chose a different system from UNICEF, the other major field network, which had already accumulated several years of experience with its own ERP.

Global perceptions

In 2010, there was a global perceptions survey undertaken of the UN development system.[15] The purpose was to obtain opinions on the relevance and effectiveness of the system from a broad representative popular constituency, of which the majority were from civil society and the private sector. The sample of over 3,200 respondents was broadly representative of all regions. Most of those to whom the survey was sent had some knowledge or experience of the UN development system; 31 percent were from the private sector, 23 percent from governments, 15 percent from nongovernmrntal organizations, 12 percent from academia, and 19 percent from the UN and other international organizations. The large majority of respondents (90 percent) were in developing countries, for whose interests the UN development system mainly works.

For agency effectiveness, the highest rated were: UNICEF, WHO, UNDP, WFP, UNESCO, UNEP, FAO, and UNAIDS. The lowest rated were: IMO, ICAO, ECE, UNWTO, and UPU. The 'soft' sectors clearly do better than the 'hard' sectors, but the ratings are influenced by individual agency visibility (regulatory agencies like ITU, UPU, and ICAO are least visible). The UN view of itself is similar but with a wider dispersion of ratings (see Figure 5.3).

Respondents were asked to rank three factors central to UN effectiveness. UN neutrality was ranked highest, followed by staff competence and absence of alternatives to the UN (Figure 5.4). Interestingly, the UN respondents in the survey were the least convinced of the uniqueness of their services, and ranked the third factor even lower.

The survey also asked respondents to rank different development domains in terms of the perceived effectiveness of the UN system. Health, education, social policy, and gender issues were deemed to be

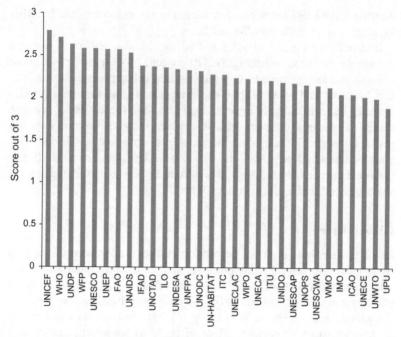

Figure 5.3 Perceived effectiveness of UN development system organizations

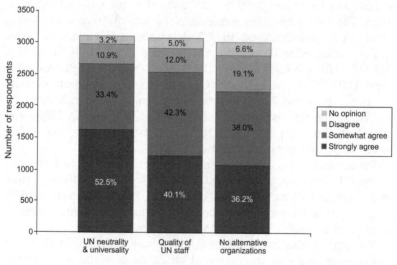

Figure 5.4 Perceived factors of UN effectiveness

the most effective, and drug control, transportation, services, and tourism the least effective. Perceptions of relevance of domain and effectiveness of agency were combined in the following chart (Figure 5.5), and here there was much greater dispersion. The large circle in the chart encloses the middling majority of organizations, in order to highlight better the most and least relevant and effective. The most valuable agencies were considered to be WHO, UNICEF, and UNAIDS. The least valuable were UN WTO (tourism), IMO (shipping), ICAO (civil aviation), UPU (postal services), and some of the regional commissions.

The clear impression from the survey is that the UN's development strengths lie in the social domain, and in education and health in particular. Although the analysis of the survey results discounts the "don't knows," perceptions are obviously influenced by visual evidence of the different agencies, and it is to be expected that the less visible tasks of standards and norm-setting will get less recognition. The findings of the survey are nevertheless of sufficient interest to have merited an exercise of asking "we, the peoples" for their views on the system, rather than only relying on the major stakeholders from within

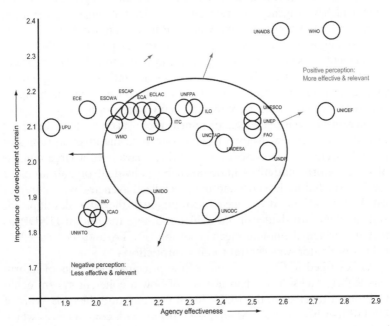

Figure 5.5 Effectiveness and relevance of UN development system organizations
Source: FUNDS perception survey 2010

member states, which have been the arbiters—and non-implementers—of the many reform proposals that have been developed over the years. These are reviewed next.

The long history of reform

The formal guidelines which defined the UN development system were meager. Chapter IX of the UN Charter on "international economic and social cooperation" set out three encompassing objectives for the UN (cited in Chapter 1 above). Chapter X established the 54-member Economic and Social Council (ECOSOC) which was intended to be the main oversight mechanism.[16] The scope of ECOSOC's work was only sparsely described and the specialized agencies were to be "brought into relationship with the United Nations," but there was little to define what that relationship was, beyond reporting regularly to ECOSOC.

The vagueness of the blueprint need not have mattered, however. Indeed the Charter left wide open the opportunity for the Secretary-General to develop a more detailed blueprint for the emerging system. One important feature was in fact instigated, and that was the "common system" of human resources management, which brought all UN staff from whichever agency or organization under the same remuneration levels and conditions of employment. But no detailed blueprint was forthcoming and an excessive degree of trust was put in ECOSOC and the General Assembly to manage the coordination role. The problem of attempting to steer this unwieldy, and constantly expanding, family of agencies was inherent and explains why concerns about bringing coherence to the system were already being raised in the 1940s.

There have been many sets of reform proposals, of which Table 5.2 provides an overview. Many of them concerned the inner workings of the UN secretariat in New York, and there have been a large number of other reform initiatives undertaken by individual organizations of the UN (including UNDP) and the specialized agencies, which are not listed. Several initiatives have also targeted the UN development system (these are shaded in the table) and here the role of UNDP, as first the principal funding mechanism for UN TA and then as a UN field coordinator, was central to all reform efforts.

As described in Chapter 1, one of the principal architects of reform was Robert Jackson. He had notions of how a coherent system could be brought together in the 1950s. But it was not until the early years of UNDP that his *Capacity Study* materialized, with consequences which have already been described. In essence, a radical but realizable set of proposals were watered down into a consensus which updated the

Table 5.2 UN-related reform initiatives since 1960

Year	Reform initiative	Source	Focus
1961	Review of the Activities and Organization of the Secretariat	Group of experts	Advocated improved representation of Socialist countries in UN staff
1966	Examination of the Administrative and Budgetary Procedures of the UN	Working group	Proposals in response to UN financial crisis
1969	Examination of the Finances of the UN and the Specialized Agencies	Group of experts	Proposed a more integrated planning and budgeting system
1969	A Study of the Capacity of the United Nations Development System (Jackson Report) (Geneva: UN, 1969)	Robert Jackson and group of experts	Commissioned by UNDP to propose a more rational and integrated development system
1969	Partners in Development (Pearson Commission)	Commission on International Development	Commissioned by World Bank to propose a strategy for increased international cooperation and development assistance
1975	A New United Nations Structure for Global Economic Cooperation ("Gardner Report")	Group of experts	Proposed new approaches in context of North-South tensions; proposed a post of UN Director General
1980	North-South: A Programme for Survival (London: Pan Books, 1980)	Independent Commission on International Development Issues (Brandt Commission)	Concerned with UN fragmentation, proposed better coordination and efficiency and reduced bureaucracy. Advocated "massive transfers" of resources from North to South

(*continued on next page*)

Table 5.2 (continued)

Year	Reform initiative	Source	Focus
1982	Common Security: A Programme for Disarmament (Palme Report)	Independent Commission on Disarmament and Security Issues	Against background of nuclear arms proliferation, proposed new arrangements for collective security
1983	Common Crisis: North-South Cooperation for World Recovery (London: Pan Books, 1983)	Brandt Commission	Made proposals to address global crises in trade, energy, food and finance
1986	Efficiency of the Administrative and Financial Functioning of the United Nations (UN Document A/41/49)	High-Level Intergovernmental expert group (Group of 18)	In context of financial crisis, proposed economies and new budget process
1987	Our Common Future (Brundtland Report)	World Commission on Environment and Development	Developed concept of "sustainable development" linking environment and energy to the development process
1992	Five Major Areas of Reform	"Wilenski Group" of 30 ambassadors	Proposed more transparent staff appointments and rationalization of UN secretariat structure
	Review of the Panel of Independent High-Level Experts	Group of experts led by Jan Pronk and Enrique Iglesias	Advised the SG on secretariat restructuring

Table 5.2 (continued)

Year	Reform initiative	Source	Focus
1993	Financing an Effective United Nations	Independent advisory group led by Shijuro Ogata and Paul Volker	Proposed new financing arrangements to prevent crises as a result of late payments to the UN
1995	Report of the Open-Ended High-Level Working Group on the Strengthening of the UN system	High-level working group	Modest proposals to streamline secretariat structure
	The United Nations in its Second Half Century	Working Group on the Future of the UN System	Addressed problems of UN credibility and proposed institutional reform (Security Council, ECOSOC)
	Our Global Neighbourhood (Oxford: Oxford University Press, 1995)	Commission on Global Governance (chaired by Ingvar Carlsson and Shridath Ramphal)	Proposed Security Council reform, economic security council, civil society involvement in UN governance, closure of some agencies and organizations
1997	Global Vision, Local Voice (General Assembly document A/AC.198/1997/CRP.1)	Task Force on Reorientation of UN Public information Activities	Proposed strengthening of information strategy and dissemination
	Renewing the United Nations: A Programme for Reform *(New York: UN, GA document A/51/950, 14 July 1997)*	Maurice Strong and group of experts	Proposed Deputy SG post, UN Development Group, reform of secretariat and working methods of its main bodies

(continued on next page)

Table 5.2 (continued)

Year	Reform initiative	Source	Focus
1999	The Report on the Panel on United Nations Peace Operations ("Brahimi Report") (A/55/305 - S/2000/809)	Expert panel led by Lakhdar Brahimi	Recommends changes in peacekeeping strategy, doctrine and operations
2004	A More Secure World: Our Shared Responsibility (A/59/565, December 2004)	High-level Panel on Threats, Challenges and Change	Established in the aftermath of the Iraq invasion, proposed reforms to intergovernmental and secretariat functions, including a Peace-Building Commission and reform of the Human Rights Council
	Report on UN-Civil Society Relations	High-level panel led by Henrique Cardoso, former president of Brazil	Proposed better access to the UN for civil society organizations
2005	Investing in Development: A Practical Plan to Achieve the Millennium Development Goals	UN Millennium Project led by Jeffrey Sachs	Proposed strengthened UN system coordination at global and country levels to support the achievement of the MDGs
2006	Delivering as One (A/61/583, 20 November 2006)	High-level Panel on UN System-wide Coherence in the areas of development, humanitarian assistance and environment	Proposed a harmonized system of programming and delivery by the UN development system at country level ("One UN"); creation of a single department in the UN for gender affairs

Table 5.2 (continued)

Year	Reform initiative	Source	Focus
	Investing in the UN: For a Stronger Organization Worldwide	Report of SG	Proposed innovations in UN secretariat (technology and financing)
	Comprehensive Review of Governance and Oversight within the UN and its Funds, Programmes and Specialized Agencies (A/60/883/Add.1 & 2, 28 August 2006)	Steering Committee	Proposed a strengthening of UN secretariat management and oversight functions
2007	The Four Nations Initiative on Governance and Management of the UN	Group of Ambassadors	Proposed more transparency in management and budget of the UN secretariat

nature of the relationship between UNDP and its "executing agencies." In 1975, a new group of 25 experts was convened, largely at the behest of the developing countries (G77). Their report (written mainly by Richard N. Gardner, a professor at Columbia University) put the choices for the UN quite starkly: "in one direction lies the prospect of new capacity to cope with the central issues facing mankind. In the other lies the danger of decline in the effectiveness of the UN."[17]

The report fell like lead onto the 38th floor of the UN. The then UN Secretary-General (Kurt Waldheim) had very little interest in reform and saw only obstacles in implementing the proposals.[18] None of the prescriptions since then have questioned fundamentally the governance or functioning of UNDP and the agencies, and all have been preoccupied mainly with coherence.

Discouragingly, it was another 20 years before serious reform of the UN system was considered again, and it came in the form of a prestigious independent commission, originally the brain-child of Willy Brandt, former German chancellor, whose own commissions had contributed to the North–South debate in the early 1980s.[19] The Commission on Global Governance, chaired by Ingvar Carlsson (former prime minister of Sweden) and Shridath Ramphal (former secretary-general of the Commonwealth), produced a report called *Our Global Neighbourhood*.[20] The value of this report was its examination of the whole concept of global governance and multilateralism, and the emerging global challenges. Much of the report deals with the UN, Bretton Woods institutions, and WTO,[21] and there is a major chapter on reforming the UN. The report calls for ECOSOC to be wound up and replaced by an economic security council and, for the first time, the efficacy of some parts of the UN development system was called into question. The commission recommended the winding up of UNCTAD and UNIDO which had outlived their usefulness: "it is important for the UN system to demonstrate a capacity not merely to change its ways of doing things within ever-widening institutional structures, but from time to time shut down institutions that can no longer be justified."[22] It also questioned the need for the five UN regional commissions, "whose continuing utility now needs to be closely examined,"[23] and suggested that the resources expended on them could be rechanneled to other regional and sub-regional organizations set up by countries (often, it should be said, without the assistance of the UN). The report urged that UNDP's role be enhanced "as the lead development agency within the UN system."[24]

Ingvar Carlsson, who was still Swedish premier when the report was published, convened a group of 16 heads of government in order to give some momentum to the proposed reforms. After Boutros-Ghali was replaced as Secretary-General at the beginning of 1997, the group approached Kofi Annan to urge action on the proposals. The timing was not propitious and the hard decisions were not taken. The reaction of the agencies targeted for extinction successfully galvanized the G77 into a counter-offensive, which construed the commission's proposals as anti-South (and subsequently voted for increases in their budgets). However, the concerns of the commission, and the emphasis it had placed on global security, probably eased the way to some changes, including notably the creation of the International Criminal Court in 2002.

The commission may also have helped inspire the new Secretary-General—the organization's first insider—who arrived with a reforming zeal. The first set of proposals, during Annan's first year in office, were contained in *Renewing the United Nations: a Programme for Reform* in 1997.[25] The proposals came from within the Secretariat and were the work of Maurice Strong, the Canadian businessman and philanthropist who had pioneered environmental causes in the UN over many years. Mostly they concerned the inner workings of the Secretariat, and called for consolidation and a reduction in posts. The report also proposed the formalization of clusters of UN programs and organizations into "executive committees," the most significant of which, for the UN development system, was the UN Development Group (UNDG), chaired by the UNDP Administrator, which was later to grow to include most of the development system agencies. (The others were for economic and social affairs, humanitarian affairs and peace and security.) The report also recognized that "if the objectives of the United Nations are to be fully realized, a much greater degree of concerted will and coordinated action are required throughout the system as a whole."[26] It proposed a strengthening of the capacities of the committee of all the UN heads (known euphemistically as the Administrative Committee on Coordination—later to be re-named the Chief Executives' Board) and more coherence at the field level through joint programs and single "UN houses." These ideas were important forerunners of the reforms in the following decade.[27]

In 2006—Annan's last year in office—the Secretary-General and then deputy Secretary-General (former UNDP Administrator Malloch Brown) established a high-level panel on UN system-wide coherence. It was co-chaired by three serving prime ministers (Mozambique, Norway, and Pakistan) and three former or future heads of government (Chile, Tanzania, and the United Kingdom) and was therefore highly representative of the contemporary concerns of governments. There were no representatives of the private sector or civil society, but the panel held consultations with nongovernmrntal interests. The panel's report, *Delivering as One*, was "a framework for a unified and coherent UN structure at the country level [...] matched by more coherent governance, funding and management arrangements at the centre."[28] During its deliberations some of the panel's more innovative draft proposals were watered down under pressure from governments and UN agencies. (For example, a group of 13 developed countries—most of the major donors to the UN development system—called again for the closing of UNCTAD, but this was opposed by the developing countries[29]) However, even the more modest recommendations (see Box 5.2) have had limited impact. The timing was again awkward. The report reached the General Assembly at a time of transition from a reformist to a much more cautious Secretary-General. Another obstacle was the conservatism of the G77 countries, whose official representatives in the UN have traditionally been suspicious of change, and may indeed be the main impediments to UN system reform.

Three of the recommendations have, however, been implemented, at least partially. The first has helped to create (by the end of 2010) eight One UN "pilots" in Albania, Cape Verde, Mozambique, Pakistan, Rwanda, Tanzania, Uruguay, and Vietnam. This is fewer than half the 2009 target, but is a first step toward greater country-level coherence. For these countries, One UN multi-donor trust funds have been established in order to encourage pooling. However, as of 2008, these trust funds had not yet become significant sources of program funding. Another concern derives from the costs of joint programming. A UNDG report of 2008 found that for participating agencies there were higher costs associated with joint programs in which they were involved.[30] There has also been a tendency to involve as many agencies as possible in joint activities in order to ensure "fair shares"—a problem which UNDP's David Owen was attempting to combat in the 1950s—and to give different agencies separate components of programs which then resemble bundle of projects requiring careful coordination.

A second partially implemented recommendation has been the establishment of "MDG" trust funds. The only current example is the $700 million "MDG Achievement Fund" provided to UNDP by the Spanish government in 2006. However, it is "multi-bilateral" funding, since it is intended only for the 59 countries of interest to the donor, which also establishes the development themes of the funding windows. The third recommendation which has been fully implemented, however, is the creation in 2010 of "UN Women" intended to consolidate into a single entity the different women's programs of the UN (including UNDP's UNIFEM). As a demonstration of the difficulty of reform

Box 5.2 Recommendations of the High-Level Panel on UN System-wide Coherence

1   Establishment of One United Nations at the country level, with one leader, one program, one budget and, where appropriate, one office (five One UN pilots initially, 20 by 2009, 40 by 2012)
2   Establishment of a Sustainable Development Board to oversee the One UN country programs
3   Appointment of a Development Coordinator, with responsibility for the performance and accountability of UN development activities
4   Establishment of an independent task force to further eliminate duplication within the UN system and consolidate UN entities, where necessary
5   Establishment of a Millennium Development Goals funding mechanism to provide multi-year funding for the One UN country programs as well as for agencies that are performing well
6   UN organizations committed to and demonstrating reform to receive full, multi-year core funding
7   Enhancement of UN role in responding to humanitarian disasters and emergencies (several proposals)
8   The UN Environment Programme to be upgraded and given real authority as the environmental policy pillar of the UN system (several proposals)
9   Establishment of one dynamic UN entity focused on gender equality and women's empowerment
10 UN Secretary-General, World Bank President, and IMF Managing Director to set up a process to review, update, and conclude formal agreements on their respective roles and relations at the global and country levels.

Source: Secretary-General's High-Level Panel on UN System-wide Coherence, *Delivering as One* (New York: UN, 2007)

through the current channels, it took four years of protracted debate—mostly about processes rather than substance—for the new body to be endorsed. In 2011, a strong Executive Director (Michelle Bachelet, the former president of Chile) was appointed at the under-secretary-general level. (It can still be debated, however, whether a cross-cutting development concern like gender equality is better promoted by a single entity, as opposed to being mainstreamed within several.)

Why reform fails

In sum, the high-level panel of 2006—the latest attempt to reform the UN system—has had limited consequences, in spite of the authoritative credentials of its membership. It leads to the rather despondent conclusion that effective reform to the system has become almost impossible. Before reviewing what potential avenues for change may lie ahead, it is instructive to list some of the reasons why reform efforts fall short.

"Intergovernmental gridlock"

This is, for Malloch Brown, the main roadblock to reform.[31] The conservatism of the government representatives in UN bodies has already been mentioned. Unfortunately, given the consensual nature of the UN general assembly and other UN governance bodies, any remotely radical proposals tend to be rejected or reduced to a lowest common denominator.

The question then arises: should government representatives in UN bodies be the main—and essentially the sole—arbiters of reform proposals? It might be more productive and meaningful if the opinions of civil society and other representatives of the intended beneficiaries of UN development cooperation could be canvassed.

UN staff

Although gridlock may occur even when the UN Secretary-General and his staff are committed to change, reform cannot move forward without drive from within. At the top of the UN Secretariat, there has traditionally been more preoccupation with the peace and security agenda than with development (in spite of which there has been no progress for many years on reforming the Security Council). Even a committed Secretary-General, whose role is to chair the Chief Executives' Board of heads of UN agencies (as well as the World Bank and IMF), would have to impose on his colleagues in any meaningful reform program. Agency heads are also defensive of the *status quo* and reluctant to sign up to reforms which could affect their own mandates or freedom of action. In this they can generally count on support from their governing bodies.

Governance arrangements

Even within the UN Organization (comprising UNDP, UNICEF, UNEP, and others), each governing body cherishes its independence. UN specialized agencies are still more autonomous. Although the same governments are represented on the many different governing bodies of the UN system, they tend to place the interests of each body above broader concerns of system-wide coherence. And UN staff are ready to influence the opinions of government delegates, to encourage an expansion of mandates, or if they feel that change is against their interests (as occurred with the demise of the UN integrated offices in Eastern Europe in 1994).

Funding patterns

The core funding of the UN system—which supports the majority of the permanent staff—comes from relatively few donor countries and is provided through each of the separate governing bodies, which further encourages fragmentation since each UN entity is effectively in competition with every other for resources. There are, even now, few multi-donor multi-agency funding sources which would help to promote coherence.

Also, the fact that most of the core funding comes from a limited number of donor countries means that the agendas of those countries—influenced by the need for accountability to their respective parliaments—may not coincide with the interests of the developing countries.

Parochial thinking

UNDP, like most parts of the system, has been through many of its own reforms. But, although as a system coordinator it has the least excuse, its approach has tended to be inward-looking. A recent example is the regionalization process discussed in Chapter 3, which took little cognizance of the decentralized structures elsewhere in the system. Other organizations and agencies also undertake frequent reform programs, but they are similarly introverted. There is, in other words, no broader "system" thinking in the upper echelons of the various UN entities.

Absence of results-orientation

For the most part UN entities do not gauge their accountability by measurable and attributable development targets. Most of those in today's development system make legitimate claims to contribute to the achievement of the Millennium Development Goals. But specific benchmarks, which would help to measure the comparative impact of the UN development system agencies, are largely lacking, making it hard to determine effectiveness objectively. There is, moreover, no culture of performance, a lacuna which was amply demonstrated in 2008 when, at the height of the global financial crisis, the General Assembly voted for almost 100 new core posts for the benefit of several UN departments and organizations (including UNCTAD, UNDESA, and the regional commissions). The beneficiary organizations merely had to make their requests; they were not required to show the achievement of any performance targets.

Conclusion: revisiting the past

A skeptical view of the future will see the UN development system continuing along its disjointed way with diminishing effectiveness. The fundamental working principles laid down more than 60 years ago will not change; the system will resist successive waves of well-meaning reforms; and it will fail, as ever, to close down any programs or organizations in which there are palpable signs of redundancy and falling interest.

The skeptics might be right. But skepticism should not be allowed to inhibit constructive speculation about a more optimistic future for the system, and UNDP within it.

One reason for optimism is that there is a degree of consensus about a future design of the system, at least in terms of its structural configuration. It is widely agreed that it has grown too dispersed and unwieldy and needs to be more cohesive, in order to be coherent, while not compromising the capacities of the strongest and most relevant parts of the system. It also requires a strong center and a single head. Various sets of reform proposals have said the same thing. Respondents in the global perception survey mentioned above were also asked to predict the shape of the system in 2025, and more than two-thirds (70 percent) agreed that there should be fewer agencies and an overall UN development chief. More than half the respondents (57 percent) agreed that the system should be consolidated in a single location.

At country level, there have already been tentative moves toward consolidation, through the formation of country teams and the One UN pilots. But there has not yet been any debate about whether the UN should still be present in all developing countries, including those at middle-income levels. Nor has there been consideration of the appropriate mix of agencies in each country, which is currently based on the uncoordinated choices of their respective headquarters.[32] Any rational geographic configuration will also have to determine whether, or in what form, the system should maintain a regional presence, either through a clustering of country offices, or as an intermediate organizational level between the global and country levels.

The discussion about the future substantive composition, governance and financing of the development system is more complex, and necessarily more controversial. However, this book, as well as many other sources which have prescribed change in the UN, has provided some pointers in these areas. On the make-up of the system, the major question is the extent to which the UN system should continue to work across all fields where other multilateral institutions are strong and already dominant; for example, economic management, in which the World Bank and the regional development banks have considerable capacity, as well as commanding the respect of finance and economic ministries. With the ascendance of the World Trade Organization, which is coming closer to universal membership, the continuing need for UNCTAD has also been questioned,[33] and a re-merger of the International Trade Centre with WTO proposed.[34] In the infrastructure area, the IMO, ICAO, ITU, and UPU would continue their roles of standard- and norm-setting. Other sectoral agencies might also be taken over by the development banks with, for example, a merger of UNIDO into the World Bank.

The UN development system would then be focused on the so-called "soft sectors" and the environment, with staff being drawn from different agencies according to need. UNEP, which has itself become a widely dispersed set of programs, should be revamped (as the High-Level Panel of 2006 had prescribed; see Box 5.2), and relocated in a single place (if not Nairobi, where it is headquartered, then Geneva where it already has a significant presence). The new UNEP should then take primary global responsibility for global negotiations on environmental management, including climate change, energy, and water, while operations would be shared with other entities, including the World Bank which controls the new Strategic Climate Fund and the Clean Technology Fund, as well as being a partner in the Global Environment Facility. There may also need to be a new body concerned with governance (parliaments, elections, public administration) and development management encompassing the functions currently provided by UNDP and the UN secretariat.

The system could be governed by a single body, e.g. a Global Development Council, modeled on several similar proposals.[35] The Council would replace the ineffective ECOSOC—the object of so many failed reform proposals—and bring together representatives of governments at a high level. Its mandate would be to oversee global development and policy-making. Crucially, however, as the main governing body of the UN development system, it would also be empowered (in sessions attended by heads of government) to choose the heads of all the agencies, including the Bretton Woods, as advocated by a former UNDP administrator[36] (see Chapter 3). It would have a powerful subordinate body acting as its secretariat, e.g. a "development board" somewhat akin to the proposal of the 2006 High-Level Panel,[37] which would act as the executive body of the system for development operations (although not for other agency tasks like norm-setting). This body, headed by the second most senior UN official (a revisited director-general), would be responsible for apportioning responsibilities to the different parts of the system for operational TA, in accordance with the needs expressed by developing countries. The board would also oversee the network of UN field operations, which would consist of four (without Europe) or five regional centers physically based within the premises of the existing regional commissions, and a number of wholly unified country offices with a single UN head appointed by the board. The country heads (appointed at a very senior level) would be well-known development specialists with good knowledge of their countries of assignment; they would in many cases not rotate within the system, but serve for a single assignment, more like the special representatives of the Secretary-General appointed to head up peace-keeping and political missions.

Of course, there are many further details of an alternative system which have not been outlined here. However, the model proposed is based on much of the accumulated wisdom of past proposals, and is by no means original. In an almost uncanny—not to say disconcerting—sense, the model also resembles the structure of EPTA from 60 years ago, shown in Figure 1.1 (Chapter 1). Disconcerting, because it illustrates how far away, and for how long, the UN system has strayed from what was once a workable framework.

Finally, what does all this imply for the future UNDP? The answer is that UNDP will have disappeared as a development agency, to be re-born at the center of the system as the executing arm of the Council: the development board. It would be headed by a globally renowned development specialist, supported by a limited number of specialist advisors seconded from other UN agencies. It would, in other words, be the "brain" of the UN development system, in the absence of which Robert Jackson had predicted 40 years ago the system would disappear (Chapter 1). Apart from interpreting policy into operational interventions, and apportioning funds from a pooled budget, the board would oversee all field operations of the system. If the model sounds radical, it bears some resemblance to the old TAB. Importantly, it resolves the bifurcation of UNDP into a system coordinator and development agency, in favor of the former. Its development "specializations" would revolve around the complex tasks of matching a wide range of development needs to the provision of services.

The board would be responsible for apportioning "core" funds. Apart from the contributions of the traditional donors, emerging countries could be encouraged to build on their demonstrated willingness to pay for services, with more co-financing through mechanisms resembling OPEX and funds-in-trust described in Chapter 1. By having developing countries pay a larger share of UN services, the accountability of the system would be shifted toward them, and willingness to pay would be an important bellwether of quality.

A gradual change in funding patterns could open a door to organizational change, even if—and perhaps especially if—overall levels of funding through the UN development system fall. Given the persistent failures of the past, change will not occur if attempts at reform follow previous trajectories and are left to the collective judgment of the conservative stakeholders who convene as ECOSOC and the General Assembly. As the One UN experiment is proving, it is also more likely to be wrought country by country than in one global swoop. As individual countries become more significant paymasters of the system's operational activities, they will have a louder say in the nature and quality of the operational services provided by the system. These and other voices need to be drawn into the debate about the future of UN development.

Notes

Foreword by the series editors

1 Stephen Browne, *The International Trade Centre: Promoting Exports for Development* (London: Routledge, 2010).
2 Stephen Browne, *Aid and Influence: Do Donors Help or Hinder?* (London: Earthscan, 2006); *Beyond Aid: From Patronage to Partnership* (London: Ashgate, 1999); and *Foreign Aid in Practice* (London: Pinter, 1990).

Foreword by Craig Murphy

1 Statistics on: peacekeepers as of November 30, 2010, "Rankings of Military and Police Contributions to UN Operations" (www.un.org/en/peace-keeping/contributors/2010/nov10_2.pdf); civilian field staff as of December 31, 2007, UN System Chief Executives Board for Coordination, High-Level Committee on Management, *Head Count of Field Staff*, (document CEB/2008/HLCM/26), December 9, 2008, 5 (including footnote e); and head-quarters' staff as of December, 31 2009, UN System Chief Executives Board for Coordination, High-Level Committee on Management, *Personnel Statistics* (document CEB/2010/HLCM/HR/24), 10, supplemented by overlooked data on the World Bank (web.worldbank.org/WBSITE/EXTERNAL/EXTABOUTUS/0,contentMDK:20101240~menuPK:1697052~pagePK:51123644~piPK:329829~theSitePK:29708,00.html) and International Monetary Fund (www.imf.org/external/np/exr/facts/glance.htm).

Introduction

1 David Mitrany, *A Working Peace System* (Chicago: Quadrangle Books, 1966); and Ernest B. Haas, *Beyond the Nation-State* (Stanford, CA: Stanford University Press, 1964).
2 The reference was in President Truman's inaugural speech of January 1949. *US Department of State Bulletin* (Washington, DC: January 30, 1949), 123.
3 See Kelley Lee, *The World Health Organization* (London: Routledge, 2008); D. John Shaw, *Global Food and Agricultural Institutions* (London: Routledge, 2008); and J. P. Singh, *The United Nations Educational, Scientific and Cultural Organization* (London: Routledge, 2010).
4 See Peter Morgan, "Technical Assistance: Correcting the Precedents," *UNDP Development Policy Journal* 2 (December 2002): 1–22.

5 Technical assistance from the World Bank was little different. For the poorer countries, it was provided as part of long-term concessionary loans which carried a very high percentage of "grant equivalent."

6 It has been estimated that 75 percent of bilateral TA is actually spent in the donor country. See Stephen Browne, *Foreign Aid in Practice* (London: Pinter, 1990), 83.

7 Margaret Joan Anstee, *Never Learn to Type: A Woman at the United Nations*, (Chichester, UK: John Wiley, 2004), 242.

8 Olav Stokke, *The UN and Development: From Aid to Cooperation*, UN Intellectual History Project (Bloomington: Indiana University Press, 2009), 485.

9 A focus on aid resources also distracted attention from some of the more important divisions between North and South, including in particular the unfairness of the international trade system. See Michael G. Schechter, *United Nations Global Conferences* (London: Routledge, 2005).

10 Kunibert Raffer and Hans Singer, *The Foreign Aid Business* (Cheltenham, UK: Edward Elgar, 1996).

11 *Analysis of the Funding of the Operational Activities for Development of the United Nations System for 2008* (ECOSOC document E/2010/76), May 14, 2010, 21.

12 The FUNDS Project, "Fact Book on the UN Development System" (Geneva: The FUNDS Project, 2010), www.fundsproject.org/?p=270. This number corresponds to the country and regional offices of the UN development system. For the UN system as a whole (including humanitarian and peacekeeping operations), there are 1,404 country and regional offices.

1 The origins of UNDP

1 The UN General Assembly resolutions calling for the establishment of EPTA and the Special Fund were the previous year in each case.

2 Mahyar Nashat, *National Interests and Bureaucracy versus Foreign Aid* (Geneva: Tribune Editions, 1978).

3 Gilbert Rist, *A History of Development* (New York: Zed Books, 1997), 65. After the Second World War, the first UNDP resident representative did not arrive in China until 1989.

4 Leon Gordenker, *The UN Secretary-General and Secretariat*, 2nd edition (London: Routledge, 2010).

5 Yet in 1948, Congress approved the Marshall Plan, one of the largest ever assistance programs, which was offered to (but refused by) the Eastern Bloc countries.

6 Richard Jolly, *UNICEF* (London: Routledge, 2011).

7 See Hugh L. Keenleyside, *International Aid: A Summary* (New York: Heinemann, 1966), 115–16.

8 United Nations, (ECOSOC resolution 222(IX)).

9 US Department of State Bulletin (Washington, DC: January 30, 1949), 123.

10 Quoted in Sixten Heppling, *UNDP: From Agency Shares to Country Programmes* (Stockholm: Ministry of Foreign Affairs, 1995), 48.

11 Resident representatives were first recruited by the UN's Technical Assistance Administration and in 1952 came under the authority of David Owen and the TAB.

12 Keenleyside, *International Aid*, 189.
13 Singer had studied with Joseph Schumpeter in Vienna and was supervised for his PhD by John Maynard Keynes in Cambridge before joining the UN.
14 Keenleyside, *International Aid*, 274.
15 Katherine Marshall, *The World Bank: From Reconstruction to Development to Equity* (London: Routledge, 2008).
16 Craig N. Murphy, *The United Nations Development Programme: A Better Way* (Cambridge: Cambridge University Press, 2006), 64–65; and John Toye and Richard Toye, *The UN and Global Political Economy: Trade, Finance and Development*, UN Intellectual History Project (Bloomington: Indiana University Press, 2004), 172.
17 General Assembly resolution 1240 (XIII), October 1958.
18 Murphy, *The United Nations Development Programme*, 65.
19 Keenleyside, *International Aid*, 261.
20 See Stephen Browne, *Aid and Influence: Do Donors Help or Hinder?* (London: Earthscan, 2006).
21 Hugh Keenleyside, who was the Director of the UN's Technical Assistance Administration, *International Aid*, 164.
22 David Blelloch, *Aid for Development* (London: Fabian Society, 1958), 39.
23 Yonah Alexander, *International Technical Assistance Experts: A Case Study of the UN Experience* (New York: Praeger, 1966), 16–17.
24 Mahyar Nashat, *National Interests and Bureaucracy versus Foreign Aid*, 138–39.
25 General Assembly resolution 1768 (XVII), November 1962.
26 Sixten Heppling, *UNDP: From Agency Shares to Country Programmes*, 70.
27 ECOSOC resolution 1020 (XXXVII) and General Assembly resolution 2929 (XX).
28 Murphy, *The United Nations Development Programme*, 57.
29 Pearson Report: Commission on International Development, *Partners in Development* (New York: Praeger, 1969).
30 Sir Robert Jackson was also one half of a formidable development couple. His wife Dame Barbara Ward was, among other things, one of the principal initiators and authors of the Pearson Report. Her report preceded Jackson's by a few months.
31 Robert G. A. Jackson, *The Case for an International Development Authority* (Syracuse, NY: Syracuse University Press, 1959). The following year, the World Bank set up the International Development Association (*sic*), which has subsequently played many of the same roles intended by Jackson's IDA.
32 Quoted in Murphy, *The United Nations Development Programme*, 142.
33 Margaret Joan Anstee, *Never Learn to Type: A Woman at the United Nations* (Chichester, UK: John Wiley, 2004), 241.
34 *A Study of the Capacity of the United Nations Development System* (Geneva: United Nations, 1969), DP/5.
35 Anstee, *Never Learn to Type*, 242.
36 Sixten Heppling was one of Jackson's collaborators in the Capacity Study and his book is titled *UNDP: From Agency Shares to Country Programmes*.
37 James Raymond Vreeland, *The International Monetary Fund: Politics of Conditional Lending* (London: Routledge, 2007).
38 *Capacity Study*, Volume II, chapter 7.
39 *Capacity Study*, Volume II, paras 148–53.

40 There were also rumors circulating in New York about Jackson (an Australian) wishing to replace Hoffman—then 79 years old—as the UNDP Administrator. Jackson, it seems, had no such ambitions, and even if he had had, the United States did not relinquish its hold on the post until 1999, when the first non-US national was appointed.

41 *Capacity Study*, Volume I, para. 31.

42 Murphy, *The United Nations Development Programme*, 145.

43 UNDP, Report of the Governing Council: Tenth Session (9–30 June 1970), 70/34 and Eleventh Session (14 January–2 February 1971), 71/14.

44 Anstee, *Never Learn to Type*, 262.

45 A more propitious time for unification is suggested by the comments of Lord Boyd Orr, Director General of FAO, who wrote in a letter to Robert Jackson (then Assistant Secretary-General for UN Coordination) in 1948: "I earnestly hope that you will be able to do what I have been clamouring for in the last two years—bring the heads of the specialized agencies together, and try to get a coordinated drive." Quoted in the *Capacity Study*, footnote on page 33.

46 "I had a feeling that bright people felt let down because there wasn't enough to do [...] we did not have much substance. [...] apart from the governance being overburdened, the day-to-day work was also overburdened. There were too many mechanisms created for dealing with what was not that much to deal with." I. G. Patel, interview with Yves Berthelot, UN Intellectual History Project, March 9, 2001.

47 "New Dimensions in Technical Cooperation," General Assembly resolution 3405 (xxx), November 28, 1975.

48 Dennis Dijkzeul, *Reforming for Results in the UN System: A Study of UNOPS* (Basingstoke, UK: Macmillan, 2000), 27.

49 UNDP Division of Finance, "Chronology of events on financial liquidity crisis – 1975" (internal memo, November 28, 1975); and *Financial Review of UNDP Resources And Programme Costs, 1972–76* (UNDP Governing Council document DP/155), January 1976.

50 However, the major growth in resources available to UN organizations has been earmarked by donors for specific purposes and destinations.

51 Murphy, *The United Nations Development Programme*, 64.

52 UNDP, *Annual Report: Delivering on Commitments* (New York: UNDP, May 2010).

53 UNDP, *UNV: Annual Report of the Administrator*, (UNDP Executive Board document DP/2010/28), June 21–July 2, 2010.

54 Olav Stokke, *The UN and Development: From Aid to Cooperation*, UN Intellectual History Project (Bloomington: Indiana University Press, 2009), 239.

55 See United Nations, *The UN and Somalia, 1992–1996*, Blue Books Series, Volume VII (New York: UN Department of Public Information, 1996). However, there was no legitimate government of the country at the time.

56 2005 World Summit Outcome Document (General Assembly document A/60/L.1), September 15, 2005, paras 138, 139.

57 The author is grateful to the UNDP historian Craig Murphy for pointing out the reasons for this funding watershed.

58 *Yearbooks of the United Nations 1970* and *1980* (New York: UN Department of Public Information, 1970 and 1980).

59 Stokke, *The UN and Development*, 223.
60 "Restructuring of the Economic and Social Sectors of the UN System," General Assembly resolution 32/197, December 20, 1977.
61 General Assembly resolution 32/197, para. 2.
62 *Report of the Ad Hoc Committee on the Restructuring of the Economic and Social Sectors of the United Nations System*, Official Records: thirty-second session (General Assembly document A/32/34), December 1977, para. 64.
63 Kenneth Dadzie, who went on to become Secretary-General of the UN Conference on Trade and Development (UNCTAD) from 1986–1994. Several of his biographies do not even mention his tenure as Director-General.
64 "The people put into the job were not the most appropriate. We were thinking it should be somebody who was a Nobel Prize winner [...] that was the kind of level. Instead of this, there was Ken Dadzie and then Jean Ripert, both admirable and dedicated men but not exactly visionaries or strong leaders." Joan Margaret Anstee, *UN Voices*, interview with Thomas G. Weiss, UN Intellectual History Project, December 14, 2000.
65 *Report of the Ad Hoc Committee on the Restructuring of the Economic and Social Sectors of the United Nations System*, para. 34.
66 See Yves Berthelot, ed., *Unity and Diversity in Development Ideas: Perspectives from the UN Regional Commissions*, UN Intellectual History Project (Bloomington: Indiana University Press, 2004), 45. "The relationship between global and regional entities that was evoked in the debate surrounding the creation of the commissions has continued to preoccupy delegations and secretariats without, however, leading to an effective division of labor."
67 See Murphy, *The United Nations Development Programme*, 167.
68 For example, during the 1970s and 1980s, UNDP in Mogadishu continued to grant long-term foreign fellowships to Somalis, from which the majority never returned.
69 See Murphy, *The United Nations Development Programme*, 261. The quote was attributed to the UNDP Administrator Bill Draper.

2 The 1980s and 1990s

1 A term coined by John Williamson in 1989: "What Washington Means by Policy Reform," in *Latin American Readjustment: How Much has Happened*, ed. John Williamson (Washington, DC: Institute for International Economics, 1989).
2 Giovanni Andrea Cornia, Richard Jolly, and Frances Stewart, eds, *Adjustment with a Human Face, Volume I: Protecting the Vulnerable and Promoting Growth* (Oxford: Clarendon Press, 1987).
3 World Bank, *Accelerated Development in Sub-Saharan Africa* (Washington, DC: World Bank, 1981). Also known as the "Berg report" after its principal author.
4 Craig N. Murphy, *The United Nations Development Programme: A Better Way?* (Cambridge: Cambridge University Press, 2006), 222.
5 See Stephen Browne and Sam Laird, *The International Trade Centre* (London: Routledge, 2011).
6 See Steve Hughes and Nigel Haworth, *The International Labour Organization: Coming in from the Cold* (London: Routledge, 2011).

7 Exemplified by the work of Robert Cassen and others at IDS Sussex. Robert Cassen and associates, *Does Aid Work?* (Oxford: Oxford University Press, 1986).

8 At different times, and for varied reasons, countries have chosen to withdraw from individual agencies and organizations of the UN. The United States withdrew from UNESCO in 1984, and the UK in 1986. During the 1990s, the United States, the UK, Germany, and Australia each withdrew from the UN Industrial Development Organization (UNIDO), and over a longer period 14 countries have withdrawn from ILO. In all cases, the countries rejoined later. The only withdrawal from UNDP has been Oman, which objected to the contents of a UNDP report.

9 *Yearbook of the United Nations 1989* (New York: UN Department of Public Information, 1990).

10 Murphy, *The United Nations Development Programme*, 214–16.

11 UNDP, *Rethinking Technical Cooperation in Africa: Reforms for Capacity Building* (New York: UNDP, 1993). One of the co-authors was Eliot Berg, also co-author of the World Bank's 1981 report on Africa.

12 Sakiko Fukuda-Parr, Carlos Lopes, and Khalid Malik, eds., *Capacity for Development: New solutions to Old Problems* (London: Earthscan, 2001); Stephen Browne, ed., *Developing Capacity through Technical Cooperation: Country Experiences* (London: Earthscan, 2002); and Carlos Lopes and Thomas Theisohn, *Ownership, Leadership and Transformation: Can We Do Better for Capacity Development?* (London: Earthscan, 2003).

13 See Richard Ponzio, *Human Development* (London: Routledge, forthcoming).

14 Murphy, *The United Nations Development Programme*, 261. The President in neighboring Sierra Leone was Ahmad Tejan Kabbah, another former UNDP staffer.

15 Murphy, *The United Nations Development Programme*, 239.

16 Mahbub ul Haq was the first to recognize the intellectual antecedents: "the rediscovery of human development is not a new invention. It is a tribute to the early leaders of political and economic thought," and he cites Aristotle and the political philosophers of the eighteenth century. Mahbub ul Haq, *Reflections on Human Development* (Oxford: Oxford University Press, 1995), 13.

17 As ul Haq was to explain later: "The defining difference between the economic growth and the human development schools is that the first focuses exclusively on the expansion of only one choice—income—while the second embraces the enlargement of all human choices—whether economic, social, cultural or political. [...] unless societies recognize that their real wealth is their people, an excessive obsession with creating material wealth can obscure the goal of enriching human lives." *Reflections on Human Development*, 14.

18 In the following year, the proxy was changed to "mean years of schooling."

19 In some regions, especially, the notion of human development was difficult to communicate. When the UNDP offices in the newly independent countries of the former Soviet Union began to proselytize the concept, they encountered widespread miscomprehension. Partly, this was the result of the exclusive Soviet planning emphasis on people as productive resources, and partly it was a linguistic problem. Human development was sometimes even translated as "pregnancy"!

20 Sakiko Fukuda-Parr, *Millennium Development Goals (MDGs): For a People-Centered Development Agenda?* (London: Routledge, forthcoming).

21 Richard Jolly, Louis Emmerij, Dharam Ghai, and Frédéric Lapeyre, *UN Contributions to Development Thinking and Practice*, UN Intellectual History Project (Bloomington: Indiana University Press, 2004), 180.

22 United Nations, *An Agenda for Development* (New York: UN, 1995).

23 *Report of the World Summit on Social Development* (UN document A/CONF.166/9), 19 April 1995.

24 Richard Jolly became the human development special adviser after ul Haq's departure.

25 http://hdr.undp.org.

26 Director of the Al-Mishkat Center for Research and Training, Egypt.

27 Rima Khalaf Hunaidi, Foreword to the *Arab Human Development Report 2002: Creating Opportunities for Future Generations* (New York: UNDP, 2002).

28 "How the Arabs Compare: Arab Human Development Report 2002," *Middle East Quarterly* 9, no. 4 (2002): 59–67.

29 Salama A. Salama, "Facing Up to Unpleasant Facts," *Al-Ahram Weekly*, July 11–17, 2002.

30 Michael Elliot, "The Trouble with Saving the World," *Time*, December 30, 2002.

31 Thomas L. Friedman, "Arabs at the Crossroads," *New York Times*, July 3, 2002.

32 Signed by every UN member country with the exception of the United States and Somalia.

33 Inge Kaul, Isabelle Grunberg, and Marc Stern, *Global Public Goods: International Cooperation in the 21st Century* (Oxford: Oxford University Press, 1999).

34 Inge Kaul, Pedro Conceição, Katell Le Goulven, and Ronald U. Mendoza, eds., *Providing Global Public Goods: Managing Globalization* (Oxford: Oxford University Press, 2003).

35 Today's ODS is described as follows: "collects up-to-date information, keeps abreast of relevant literature and policy developments, and produces research relevant to UNDP" (vacancy announcement in *The Economist*, July 10, 2010).

36 For example, a group of knowledge management experts stated in a report that "we believe UNDP has something unique going on. [...] Overall, the system is remarkable." from Tom Davenport, Steve Denning, Geoff Parcell, and Larry Prusk, "Review of UNDP's networks and communities" (New York: UNDP, 2004), unpublished paper.

37 Elizabeth R. DeSombre, *Global Environmental Institutions* (London: Routledge, 2006).

38 With the exception of negotiations on the Law of the Sea, which resulted after nine years of negotiations in a UN Convention (UNCLOS) in 1982, with a secretariat based in Jamaica.

39 Ozone depletion is caused by a build-up in the atmosphere of CFCs emitted by household appliances such as air-conditioners. A key factor of success in agreeing the Convention was the discovery of inexpensive substitutes, which persuaded all countries—including the usually reluctant United States—to ratify.

40 *Development and International Co-operation: Environment* (UN document A/42/427), March 1987, www.un-documents.net/wced-ocf.htm.

41 It is sobering to reflect that, unlike in the case of the Ozone Convention, it has not been possible under the UN Framework Convention on Climate Change, even after nearly two decades, for agreement to be reached on limiting the emissions of greenhouse gases which cause global warming, mainly because of the inability to assign realistic environmental costs (as opposed to market prices) to combustible carbons.

42 Stephen Browne, *Beyond Aid: From Patronage to Partnership* (Aldershot, UK: Ashgate, 1999), 32–37.

43 Olav Stokke, *The UN and Development: From Aid to Cooperation*, UN Intellectual History Project (Bloomington: Indiana University Press, 2009), 383.

44 Seniority was established by the fact that the Associate (i.e. deputy) Administrator was also an under-secretary-general, and that there were, additionally, eight assistant secretary-general posts in UNDP headquarters.

3 UNDP in the twenty-first century

1 When the Secretary-General failed to appoint the Danish candidate Poul Neilsen (who went on to become the Aid Commissioner in the European Commission), the Danish government cut its contribution to UNDP by 40 percent.

2 Gil Loescher, Alexander Betts, and James Milner, *UNHCR: The Politics and Practice of Refugee Protection into the Twenty-First Century* (London: Routledge, 2008).

3 "Assessing UNDP: Overview of recent surveys" (internal document), April 2005.

4 UNDP, *Delivering on Commitments: UNDP in Action 2009/2010*, Annual Report (New York: UNDP, 2010).

5 An example well-known to the author is Rwanda, one of the world's poorest countries, which, using its own resources, had already put in place an effective and inexpensive nationwide mobile telephone service in the 1990s. In a relatively uniform global market for ICTs, the huge variation in the cost and reliability of internet services in developing countries is one of the best indicators of the willingness of governments to adopt appropriate policies.

6 See, for example, Sebastian Mallaby, *The World's Banker* (New Haven, Conn.: Yale University Press, 2004).

7 World Summit for Social Development, *Copenhagen Declaration on Social Development, 1995*, especially Commitment 2, available at: www.un.org/esa/socdev/wssd/decl_partc.html. An example was Mali, where UNDP had supported the development of a national poverty strategy over two years, based on a comprehensive process of national consultation. The strategy was completed in 1998 and launched at a round-table of government ministers and donors in the same year. When the World Bank team arrived in Mali to undertake the PRSP, they pointedly ignored the strategy.

8 The first round of PRSPs bore an uncanny resemblance to the preceding Policy Framework Papers, in which the bank prescribed the economic policies that countries would need to adopt to be eligible for loans. Like the

Policy Framework Papers, the PRSPs were framed (World Bank-style) in phases of three years only, an impractically short period in which to record sustainable progress in poverty reduction. The manner in which the first PRSPs were hastily written (usually in English), mainly by teams of World Bank consultants making flying visits to each country, and then submitted to the donor-dominated Board for approval, meant that the scope for local consultation was extremely limited.

9 Also a former consultant for UNDP in Latin America and Eastern Europe.

10 UN Millennium Project, *Investing in Development: A Practical Plan to Achieve the Millennium Development Goals* (London: Earthscan, 2005), xxi and chapter 4. In fact, the setting of country-specific human development goals with long-term targets was a sounder basis for developing strategies to overcome poverty than three-year PRSPs.

11 It was a very sound recommendation. One of the criticisms of the PRSPs was that they were essentially program frameworks of only three years' duration (in keeping with World Bank lending rhythms), whereas poverty reduction was known to be a much longer-term process; and it makes much more sense to concentrate on some concrete human development goals to be achieved by a certain date. In practice, some developing countries have—confusingly—been invited to prepare both types of strategy (by the World Bank and the UN, respectively).

12 See www.un.org/esa/ffd/monterrey/MonterreyConsensus.pdf.

13 *Multi-Year Funding Framework Report on UNDP Performance and Results for 2004*, (Executive Board document DP/2005/16), May 12, 2005.

14 UNDP has established a separate office in New York to manage the large number of multi-donor trust funds that have been established to support UN activities in many countries. As discussed in a later chapter, however, the largest share of these funds (totaling some $US5 billion) are actually spent by UNDP as the implementing agency.

15 UNDP's *Human Development Report 1992* (New York: Oxford University Press, 1992) had proposed a "Development Security Council," Box 5.1, 82.

16 Kemal Derviş, *A Better Globalization: Legitimacy, Governance and Reform* (Washington, DC: Center for Global Development, 2005), 98.

17 *Delivering as One* (report of the UN Secretary-General's High-level Panel on System-wide Coherence), November 2, 2006.

18 *Delivering as One*, 11.

19 See Richard Jolly, Louis Emmerij, and Thomas G. Weiss, *UN Ideas that Changed the World*, UN Intellectual History Project (Bloomington: Indiana University Press, 2009), 32–47.

20 During Malloch Brown's time, the associate administrator had been Zéférin Diabré, a youthful former Minister of Finance from Burkina Faso. Although Diabré pre-dated Malloch Brown, his functions were essentially to deputize, and he was not given the same independent degrees of responsibility as Melkert and some of his predecessors.

21 In 2008, Spain contributed a further €90 million (US$120 million).

22 See www.mdgfund.org.

23 One of the most graphic examples is the cluster of individual UN offices in a building near Congress in Washington, the main purpose of which is to lobby for funds—not for the system as a whole, but for themselves individually.

24 Letter from Ambassador Mark D. Wallace to Ad Melkert, January 16, 2007. The letter was the basis of subsequent articles by The Heritage Foundation, *Wall Street Journal*, and other right-wing media in the United States.

25 *Report of the Executive Board of the United Nations Development Programme on its Work During 2007*, (ECOSOC Official Records, Supplement No. 15), 2007, 49–50.

26 The US Mission asked for access to internal audit reports and was initially denied access.

27 *Report of the Executive Board of the United Nations Development Programme on its Work During 2007*, 4–5 and 50–52.

28 His absence during part of the September 2007 session at which the Strategic Plan was discussed was explained by his "attending to previously scheduled commitments abroad" in the report of the meeting.

29 There is already speculation in New York about a woman as the next UN Secretary-General.

30 Conversation with the author, November 18, 2010.

31 *Composition of the Secretariat: Report of the Secretary-General*, (UN document A/64/352), September 15, 2009, 23. The figures correspond to June 2009.

32 One good example, among many, was UNDP's support to the inter-governmental Mekong Committee of four riparian states (Cambodia, Laos, Thailand, and Vietnam) during a difficult political era in Southeast Asia; the program also included the institutional strengthening of each of the four national committees.

33 *A Study of the Capacity of the United Nations Development System* (United Nations, DP/5), 1969, chapter 7.

34 UNDP, "Functional Alignment of and Implementation Arrangements for Regional Service Centres" (New York, 2008).

35 The FUNDS project, *Fact Book on the UN Development System*, www.fundsproject.org/?p=270.

36 *Regional Cooperation in the Economic, Social and Related Fields* (UN Economic and Social Council documents E/2009/15 and E/2010/15), June 2009 and June 2010.

4 Performance and results

1 The UNDP historian quotes a former staff member who preferred to say that he worked for UNICEF, rather than having to explain his own organization's focus. See Craig N. Murphy, *The United Nations Development Programme: A Better Way?* (Cambridge: Cambridge University Press, 2006), 232.

2 www.undp.org/about.

3 Olav Stokke, *The UN and Development: From Aid to Cooperation*, UN Intellectual History Project (Bloomington: Indiana University Press, 2009), 485.

4 UNDP, *Evaluation of Result-Based Management at UNDP* (New York: UNDP Evaluation Office, 2007). The report also stated that "RBM has been applied within the organization, but has had little effect on development effectiveness at the country level."

5 OECD, *2010 Development Cooperation Report* (Paris: Organization for Economic Cooperation and Development, 2010), statistical annex.

6 *Human Development Report 1990* (New York: UNDP, 1990) and *World Development Report 1990* (Washington DC: World Bank, 1990).

7 Maggie Black, *The No-Nonsense Guide to the United Nations* (Oxford: New Internationalist Publications, 2008), 79.

8 The flaws in process were referred to in the first internal review: World Bank and IMF, *Review of the PRSP Approach: Main Findings* (Washington, DC: World Bank and IMF, 2002).

9 Deepa Narayan *et al.*, *Voices of the Poor*, several volumes (Oxford: Oxford University Press, 2001–02).

10 UNIFEM is due to be wound up in 2011 with the creation of the new UN program UN Women.

11 See Murphy, *The United Nations Development Programme*, 208–9.

12 A.J. Barry, *Aid Coordination and Aid Effectiveness: A Review of Country and Regional Experience* (Paris: Organization for Economic Cooperation and Development, 1988).

13 *Annual Report 2010: Delivering on Commitments* (New York: UNDP, 2010).

14 Murphy, *The United Nations Development Programme*, 332–33.

15 UNDP Evaluation Office, *Evaluation of UNDP Assistance to Conflict-Affected Countries* (New York: UNDP, 2006). The six countries were: Afghanistan, the Democratic Republic of the Congo, Guatemala, Haiti, Sierra Leone, and Tajikistan.

16 Poor coordination in post-conflict situations prompted the establishment of the UN's peace-building commission in 2006, but to date it has been deployed in few countries.

17 *Evaluation of the Role and Contribution of UNDP in Environment and Energy* (New York: UNDP, 2008), 71.

18 *Evaluation of the Role and Contribution of UNDP in Environment and Energy.*

19 See The FUNDS project, *Fact Book on the UN Development System*, www. FundsProject.org. This process of outreach was facilitated by the donor countries, which have always provided the major part of the core funding of the UN system. While occasionally decrying the problems of proliferation and duplication in the UN, the same governments were sending representatives to the different governing bodies of the UN agencies and organizations and supporting the financing of these ever-expanding networks.

20 Recent examples of UNDP's advantage have been shown in the apportionment of resources from the multi-donor, multi-agency funds with which it has been entrusted.

21 *Delivering as One*, Report of the High-level Panel on United Nations System-wide Coherence in the areas of Development, Humanitarian Assistance and the Environment, (General Assembly document A/61/583), 20 November 2006.

22 Albania, Cape Verde, Mozambique, Pakistan, Rwanda, Tanzania, Uruguay, and Vietnam.

23 *Charter of the United Nations and Statute of the International Court of Justice* (New York: United Nations Department of Information, 1945 onwards).

24 The Board comprises 36 member countries by rotation: eight from Africa, seven from Asia, five from Latin America and the Caribbean, four from Eastern Europe, and 12 from Western Europe and North America.

25 DFID, *Assessment of Multilateral Organizational Effectiveness: An Overview of Results* (London: Department for International Development, 2005), http://webarchive.nationalarchives.gov.uk/+/www.dfid.gov.uk/pubs/files/meff-results.pdf.

26 William Easterly and Tobias Pfutze, "Where Does the Money Go? Best and Worst Practices in Foreign Aid," *Journal of Economic Perspectives* 22, no. 2 (Spring 2008).

27 Easterly and Pfutze, "Where Does the Money Go? Best and Worst Practices in Foreign Aid," 20.

28 Non-core resources—also called "multi-bilateral," extra-budgetary or earmarked contributions—are provided to UN agencies and organizations by donors, but are intended for particular purposes. Thus, while UN entities consider non-core funds to be part of their operational budgets, OECD Development Assistance Committee (OECD/DAC) donors classify them as bilateral funding.

29 In the 1990s, half of the international professional staff in UNDP's country offices in Africa were junior professional officers funded by donors.

30 The author once headed a UNDP country office that (initially) comprised 160 people (45 international professionals), of whom 20 were drivers. The total UN presence in the country was over 1,500.

31 Australia, Austria, Belgium, Canada, Denmark, Finland, France, Germany, Ireland, the Netherlands, Norway, Republic of Korea, Spain, Sweden, Switzerland, and the United Kingdom.

32 *MOPAN Common Approach: UNDP 2009*, February 19, 2010, vi. http://static.mopanonline.org/brand/upload/documents/UNDP_Final_February_19_issued_.pdf.

33 *MOPAN Common Approach: UNDP 2009*, 9.

5 The future of the UN development system

1 See The Future of the United Nations Development System (FUNDS) project: www.futureun.org or www.fundsproject.org. The goal of this project is to promote dialogue and research on a future structure of the UN development system in 2025 and beyond.

2 WIPO also had antecedents in the nineteenth century. See Christopher May, *The World Intellectual Property Organization* (London: Routledge, 2007).

3 Craig N. Murphy, *International Organization and Industrial Change* (Oxford: Polity Press, 1994), 7.

4 Mark Malloch Brown, "Can the UN Be Reformed?" *Global Governance* 14 (January–March 2008).

5 See Craig N. Murphy and JoAnne Yates, *The International Organization for Standardization: Global Governance through Voluntary Consensus* (London: Routledge, 2009).

6 See Thomas G. Weiss and Ramesh Thakur, *Global Governance and the UN: An Unfinished Journey*, UN Intellectual History Project (Indiana University Press, 2010), 20–23.

7 The World Bank overtook UNDP in the early 1980s. See Morten Boas and Desmond McNeill, *Multilateral Institutions: A Critical Introduction* (London: Pluto Press, 2003), 40.

8 OECD/DAC aid statistics, www.oecd.org/document/16/0,3343,en_2649_34447_42396496_1_1_1_1,00.html

9 See also Stephen Browne, *Aid and Influence: Do Donors Help or Hinder?* (London: Earthscan, 2006).

10 See Ian Taylor and Karen Smith, *The United Nations Conference on Trade and Development* (London: Routledge, 2007), 69.

11 Richard Jolly, Louis Emmerij, and Thomas G. Weiss, *UN Ideas that Changed the World*, UN Intellectual History Project (Bloomington: Indiana University Press, 2009), 206.

12 Thomas G. Weiss, *What's Wrong with the United Nations and How to Fix it* (Cambridge: Polity Press, 2009), 72–106.

13 Many months after the food crises of 2008, the UN system was still negotiating over the composition of its inter-agency task force.

14 As an echo of earlier attempts to develop a code of conduct for multinational corporations, the UN launched a "global compact" in 2000 inviting private enterprises to sign up to ten principles of sustainable and ethical development. This sound initiative has helped to promote greater understanding between the UN and private enterprise, but has no ramifications for the UN's own activities.

15 The survey was undertaken by The Future of the UN Development System (FUNDS) project, based in Geneva.

16 *Charter of the United Nations and Statute of the International Court of Justice* (UN Department of Public information), various years.

17 *A New United Nations Structure for Global Economic Cooperation* (Report of the Group of Experts on the Structure of the UN system, UN document E/AC.62.9), 1975.

18 Richard Gardner, the main author, described the report's reception as follows: "so we put together a pretty good report, but Kurt Waldheim was utterly cynical. He got this report, and he had no interest in our recommendations because they all involved major changes in the status quo, and he didn't see how this would serve his purpose. And he had a couple of people on the 38th floor who didn't like our proposals because it would have shaken things up, and maybe diminished their authority. So we worked our hearts out on this report and nothing happened—nothing. It was very frustrating," United Nations Intellectual History Project, *UN Voices: The Complete Oral History Transcripts*, 2007.

19 Independent Commission on International Development Issues, *North–South: A Programme for Survival* (London: Pan Books, 1980), and *Common Crisis North–South: Cooperation for World Recovery* (London: Pan Books, 2003).

20 Commission on Global Governance, *Our Global Neighbourhood* (Oxford: Oxford University Press, 1995).

21 Bernard M. Hoekman and Petros C. Mavroidis, *The World Trade Organization: Law Economics and Politics* (London: Routledge, 2007).

22 Commission on Global Governance, *Our Global Neighbourhood*, 282–83.

23 *Our Global Neighbourhood*, 290–91.

24 *Our Global Neighbourhood*, 275.

25 *Renewing the United Nations: A Programme for Reform* (UN document A/51/950), July 14, 1997.

26 *Renewing the United Nations*, 27.

27 One of the least fortunate proposals, however, from the point of view of system reform, was the creation of a post of deputy Secretary-General. The new position—essentially just to deputize the Secretary-General—effectively short-circuited the possibility of naming a director-general as number two in the hierarchy, with oversight over the entire development system. With the creation of the executive committees, the UN could, as an alternative, have designated four *de facto* deputies for each of its main fields of activity.

28 *Delivering as One* (Secretary-General's High-Level Panel on UN System-wide Coherence, UN sales number E.07.1.8), 2007, iii.

29 See Jonas von Freiesleben, "System-wide Coherence" in the Center for UN Reform Education, *Managing Change at the United Nations* (New York, 2008), 42.

30 www.undg.org/docs/10289/UNStocktakingSynthesisReportV6.pdf.

31 Mark Malloch Brown, "Can the UN Be Reformed?" *Global Governance* 14 (January–March 2008).

32 Mexico City, the capital of an OECD country, currently has over 20 regional and country UN offices, whereas in the least-developed country of Mauritania there are only six.

33 See, for example, Ian Taylor and Karen Smith, *United Nations Conference on Trade and Development (UNCTAD)* (London: Routledge, 2007).

34 Stephen Browne and Sam Laird, *The International Trade Centre* (London: Routledge, 2011). Before its formal creation in 1964, the ITC had been a division within the General Agreement on Tariffs and Trade (GATT), the forerunner of WTO.

35 For example: Mahbub ul Haq, *Reflections on Human Development* (Oxford: Oxford University Press, 1995), 164–77; and Kemal Derviş, *A Better Globalization: Legitimacy, Governance and Reform* (Washington, DC: Center for Global Development, 2005), 73–104.

36 Derviş, *A Better Globalization*, 98–99.

37 *Delivering as One*, 44–45.

Select bibliography

History

Craig N. Murphy, *The United Nations Development Programme: A Better Way* (Cambridge: Cambridge University Press, 2006). This is the only full history to have been written about UNDP. It was a labor of two years and contains a large number of examples of UNDP in action, particularly at the field level. It provides a useful complement to the present book.

Margaret Joan Anstee, *Never Learn to Type: A Woman at the United Nations* (Chichester, UK: John Wiley, 2004). Anstee was the principal author of the *Capacity Study* which carries the name of Robert Jackson (see below). She spent most of her career in the UN system, was the first woman to become a UNDP resident representative and the first to be a UN Under-Secretary-General. This autobiographical work contains many insights on UNDP and the development system, by a critical insider.

Hugh L. Keenleyside, *International Aid: A Summary* (New York: Heinemann, 1966); Yonah Alexander, *International Technical Assistance Experts: A Case Study of the UN Experience* (New York: Praeger, 1966). These two books describe the early days of UN technical assistance before the creation of UNDP.

Sixten Heppling, *UNDP: From Agency Shares to Country Programmes* (Stockholm: Ministry of Foreign Affairs, 1995). Heppling was a collaborator in Jackson's *Capacity Study* (see below), on secondment from the Swedish Ministry of Foreign Affairs. His book contains many useful insights on the relationship between UNDP and the UN agencies in the first few years of UNDP's existence.

Human development

UNDP, *Human Development Report 1990* (New York: UNDP, 1990); Mahbub ul Haq, *Reflections on Human Development* (Oxford: Oxford

University Press, 1995); Richard Jolly, Louis Emmerij, and Thomas G. Weiss, *UN Ideas that Changed the World*, UN Intellectual History Project (Bloomington and Indianapolis: Indiana University Press, 2009). There is a large literature on human development, which continues to grow. In the present series, *Human Development* is due to be published by Routledge in 2011. Apart from the first and subsequent annual human development reports, the book by ul Haq, the true father of the paradigm, contains some useful analysis of the origins of the idea and of the impact it has had on development thinking. Jolly *et al.*'s book in the UN Intellectual History Project series contains a chapter on human development, which describes how the concept helped to integrate many contemporary ideas about development.

Millennium Development Goals

"United Nations Millennium Declaration," UN General Assembly resolution 55/2, September 8, 2000; UN Millennium Project, *Investing in Development: A Practical Plan to Achieve the Millennium Development Goals* (London and Sterling: Earthscan, 2005). The MDGs were embodied in the historic declaration that emerged from the 2000 Millennium Summit. Subsequently, under the leadership of Jeffrey Sachs, the Millennium Project was established, together with a series of ten specialized task forces, which each produced detailed reports. *Investing in Development* is a useful summary of these reports and provides valuable guidance on how the MDGs could be achieved.

General development context

Olav Stokke, *The UN and Development: From Aid to Cooperation*, UN Intellectual History Project (Bloomington and Indianapolis: Indiana University Press, 2009); John Toye and Richard Toye, *The UN and Global Political Economy: Trade, Finance and Development* (Bloomington: Indiana University Press, 2004); Maggie Black, *The No-Nonsense Guide to the United Nations* (Oxford: New Internationalist Publications, 2008). These three books are about the UN in development, and provide useful contextual commentary on the role of UNDP in the larger development campaign.

Richard Jolly, Louis Emmerij, and Thomas G. Weiss, *UN Ideas that Changed the World*, UN Intellectual History Project (Bloomington: Indiana University Press, 2009). This final summative volume of the UN Intellectual History Project describes nine areas in which the UN system has made a major contribution to development thinking and action, nearly all of which are in areas of concern to UNDP. It includes separate chapters on human development and development goals (including the MDGs).

Performance

Stephan Klingebiel, *Effectiveness and Reform of the United Nations Development Programme* (London: Frank Cass, 1999). This comprehensive PhD thesis provides a thorough review of the challenges facing UNDP and the reform processes of the 1990s.

Department for International Development, *Assessment of Multilateral Organizational Effectiveness: An Overview of Results* (London: DFID, 2005); William Easterly and Tobias Pfutze, "Where Does the Money Go? Best and Worst Practices in Foreign Aid," *Journal of Economic Perspectives* 22, no. 2 (2008): 29–52. These two assessments of the performance of development agencies, including UNDP, use different criteria and arrive at very different results. In the former, UNDP is rated very highly; in the latter, it is ranked low. Both provide useful analysis, but are examples of the perils of agency performance ratings.

Reform

A Study of the Capacity of the United Nations Development System, (document DP/5), 1969; *Renewing the United Nations: A Programme for Reform*, (General Assembly document A/51/950), July 14, 1997; and the Secretary-General's High-Level Panel on UN System-wide Coherence, *Delivering as One* (E.07.1.8), 2007. There have been many works on UN reform, in part because rather little has fundamentally changed in the system over many years. These three reports were specifically commissioned by the system and contain the most significant proposals for strengthening the UN development system. The first is the classic *Capacity Study* of 1969, which this book describes in some detail, and which may be considered to have been the last chance for radical reform. The two more recent reports were equally authoritative and contain realistic proposals, which have been only very partially implemented.

Brian Urquhart and Erskine Childers, *Towards a More Effective United Nations* (Uppsala, Sweden: Dag Hammarskjöld Foundation, 1992); Erskine Childers and Brian Urquhart, *Renewing the United Nations System* (Uppsala, Sweden: Dag Hammarskjöld Foundation, 1994); Commission on Global Governance, *Our Global Neighbourhood*

(Oxford: Oxford University Press, 1995). Urquhart and Childers were two insiders who teamed up to produce their own sets of proposals for UN system reform. These books provide useful commentary on the stop–go reform processes in the 1980s and 1990s.

Websites

Much improved and upgraded in recent years, UNDP's central site, www.undp.org, makes it easy to navigate to each of the sites of the UNDP country offices and from there to the sites of the UN country teams. Many of these country-based sites, however, are in French (West Africa) or Spanish (Latin America) only. The central site also provides access to the Human Development Indicators.

The best development system site is that of the UN Development Group: www.undg.org. Browsing this site gives a good idea of the highly elaborate mechanisms and procedures that have been established to improve development system coordination.

Each of the entities of the UN development system has well-designed sites, such as:

www.unicef.org
www.wfp.org
www.unfpa.org
www.who.int
www.unesco.org
www.ilo.org
www.fao.org
www.unido.org

The website of the UN Intellectual History Project, www.unhistory. org, provides information on the ten-year project which has generated 17 volumes on the UN system as well as "oral histories" from 79 key UN personalities.

Index